Martha Frances

Praise for *Inner Peace for Busy People*

❧❧ ❧❧ ❧❧

"Joan Borysenko is the quintessential Queen of Enlightenment. Her wit and wisdom are astounding! Forget all the psychobabble of the last decade. At last a book that helps us destress, renew, and rejoice in our lives—written by a brilliant scholar, scientist, and psychologist. I love Joan, her mind, and her book—and so will you."
— **Loretta LaRoche**, author of *Life Is Not a Stress Rehearsal*, and star of PBS television

"Whenever I read a book, I always underline the parts I particularly like. I ran out of ink with this one! What a delight this book is: helpful, sane, wise, and witty. As Joan well says, our days 'can become a burdensome exercise in simply getting things done, slogging through a swamp of responsibilities.' God bless Joan for giving us such a useful map for getting out of the swamp."
— **Richard N. Bolles**, author of *What Color Is Your Parachute?*

*"In her new book, **Inner Peace for Busy People**, Joan Borysenko delivers the one thing every busy person longs for— simple strategies to reduce stress and create a more peaceful mind. Written in Joan's warm and humorous style, the practical wisdom and easy-to-do exercises in this book will change your life!"*
— **Cheryl Richardson**, author of *Take Time for Your Life* and *Life Makeovers*

INNER PEACE
FOR BUSY PEOPLE

Other Hay House Titles of Related Interest

Books

A Deep Breath of Life, by Alan Cohen
How to Get from Where You Are to Where You Want to Be,
by Cheri Huber
"I'd Change My Life If I Had More Time,"
by Doreen Virtue, Ph.D.
Inner Wisdom, by Louise L. Hay
Life Lessons and Reflections, by Montel Williams
Meditations, by Sylvia Browne
Sound Choices, by Susan Mazer and Dallas Smith (CD included)

Audio Programs

Change Your Thoughts, Change Your Life, by Louise L. Hay
Discovering and Recovering Your Creative Self,
by Julia Cameron and Mark Bryan
Igniting Your Soul Life, by Gary Zukav
Meditations for Difficult Times, by Bernie Siegel, M.D.
There Is a Spiritual Solution to Every Problem,
by Dr. Wayne W. Dyer

༉ ༉ ༉

All of the above are available at your local bookstore,
or may be ordered through Hay House, Inc.:

(800) 654-5126 or **(760) 431-7695**
(800) 650-5115 (fax) or **(760) 431-6948 (fax)**
www.hayhouse.com

INNER PEACE
FOR BUSY PEOPLE

52 Simple Strategies
for Transforming Your Life

JOAN BORYSENKO, PH.D.

Hay House, Inc.
Carlsbad, California • Sydney, Australia

Published and distributed in the United States by:
Hay House, Inc., P.O. Box 5100, Carlsbad, CA 92018-5100
(800) 654-5126 • (800) 650-5115 (fax) • www.hayhouse.com

Editorial supervision: Jill Kramer • *Design:* Summer McStravick

Library of Congress Cataloging-in-Publication Data

Borysenko, Joan.
    Inner peace for busy people : 52 simple strategies for transforming your life / Joan Borysenko
        p. cm.
    ISBN 1-56170-870-4
    1. Peace of mind. I. Title.

BF637. P3 B67 2001
158.1—dc21

                                                            2001024157

ISBN 1-56170-870-4

04 03 02 01   4 3 2 1
1st printing, July 2001

Printed in the United States of America

CONTENTS

ᔕ 🦋 ᔕ

PART VI: STRATEGIES FOR CREATING WISDOM
AND PURPOSE IN YOUR LIFE

Acknowledgments

If it takes a village to raise a child, it takes a world to write a book. Every author's wisdom and insight grows out of gifts given by an enormous number of people. Over the years, I've had the pleasure of working closely with several colleagues, often referred to in these pages.

Cheryl Richardson, author and head of Oprah's coaching team, is a wonderful friend and a great inspiration. She is a veritable font of practical advice. Her consistent emphasis on taking small steps to reach your goal is one of the strongest threads woven through this book. And without the retreat we facilitated together at the Miraval Spa in Tucson, Arizona, I wouldn't have had the Equine Experience that was an elegant summary of everything I teach.

Tremendous thanks to my dear friend—author, humorist, and Public Television personality Loretta LaRoche. Her knowledge of cognitive psychology is surpassed only by her brilliant and zany sense of humor. The wisdom of "Her Holiness, The Jolly Lama," has invaded my brain. While I've tried to credit all of her contributions, some of her nutty nuggets may have slipped past my radar, straight from the brain graft onto the page. I can't tell anymore. I'm menopausal.

Janet Quinn is another colleague whose wisdom and kindness live inside me. A nurse, professor, psychotherapist, research scientist, and one of the pioneers of Therapeutic Touch, Janet is the most compassionate person I know. She is my teacher of love, and one of the most evident blessings of this life. Her wise story about the camel is credited in the text. Her friendship, which has been a precious crucible for my growth, pervades every page between the lines.

Robin Casarjian, author and director of the Lionheart Foundation, is another dear and precious friend. She is my teacher of forgiveness, and every word you read here about that important subject was her gift. Robin's love and support have kept me afloat in many *dark* times, and have been a source of joy in *all* times.

Elizabeth Lawrence, my friend and partner in the Gathering of Women retreats, is the ghost in the machine. As with Loretta, Janet, and Robin, we've worked together for so long, and shared so much, that it's sometimes hard to tell her wisdom from my own. I thank her for all the ways, hidden and revealed, that she has supported and loved me, contributing to this book and to my life.

Jon Kabat-Zinn, author and director of the Center for Mindfulness in Medicine, Health Care, and Society at the University of Massachusetts Medical School, first introduced me to mindfulness as an important component of stress reduction in the 1980s. My life is richer because of his wisdom, as are the lives of the thousands of people who have attended the many mindfulness-based stress reduction and relaxation programs he has spawned in the United States and abroad.

The friendship and collegiality of psychologist Chris Hibbard, our shared interests in mind/body medicine, and her uncanny ability to create family are blessings that have added so much to my work and to my life. "Dr. Donna," thanks for helping me fill the well back up.

Celia Thaxter Hubbard has been a spiritual sounding board, a mother when my own passed away, a generous friend of the heart, and a partner in many grand adventures.

That this book exists at all is a tribute to Reid Tracy, vice president of Hay House, my publisher. Reid's constant support over the years, his faith in me, and his willingness to support new ventures is the reason that I call him my Guardian Angel.

Through Reid's generosity and tireless efforts, I was given the opportunity to create a Public Television Pledge Special, which has the same name as this book. The book, the special, and the music CD created in partnership with Don Campbell that comprise the *Inner Peace in a Busy World* package are all Reid's doing.

Thanks to my literary agent extraordinaire, Ned Leavitt. He has seen me through several books and numerous other projects with great advice, love, and understanding.

Niki Vittel, the producer of the Public Television counterpart to this book, has a sharp mind, a big heart, and a fabulous sense of humor. Niki helped me hone my ideas and refine the content of the book. She was a clear mirror in which I could better see the impact of the stories. She was also the book's first reader. The fact that she loved it gave me the energy I needed to go back and make it even better.

Don Campbell, author of *The Mozart Effect* and *The Mozart Effect for Children*, is a dear friend and an incredible musician. He cooked up the idea for the *Inner Peace for Busy People* classical music CD, and labored hard in the midst of his very busy world to make it happen. Among many other gifts, Don recognized Ralph Vaughan Williams's remarkable composition, *The Lark Ascending,* as my soul's song. Bill Howardell of Spring Hill Media produced our fabulous CD, and he is a genius to whom I owe many warm thanks.

Jill Kramer, my editor at Hay House, is always a pleasure to work with. A great editor is the invisible hand that takes a rough sculpture and turns it into art. I thank her for her sure hand.

I am deeply grateful to my crackerjack assistant, Luzie Mason. She keeps everything going with her commitment to service in its truest sense. And to my other fabulous helpers—Kathleen Gilgannon, Amelia Schreiber, and Nancy Mason—thanks a million. You make it all possible.

Finally, I am grateful to my husband, Kurt Kaltreider. Thanks for the love, the home cooking, the deep conversations, the golf, the walks, the books, the music, the ceremonies, the prayers—and especially, all the laughter.

︎ ☙

(**Author's Note:** Stories about people whose names are not in quotation marks are used with their permission. I thank each one of you who shared a little bit of your life with me. Stories in which only a first name surrounded by quotation marks is used are either true accounts in which names and any identifying details have been changed to protect confidentiality, or are composites drawn from years of working with people. The latter are true to the spirit of the teaching, although not to the experience of any particular person.)

ᝈ ᝈ ᝈ

Introduction

My husband, Kurt, and I live on a quiet mountaintop in a sleepy Colorado town where there are almost as many dogs as there are people. Our own four canines, ranging in size from a petite Maltese to a noble collie, are part of the local fauna. They love to run in the spruce- and pine-filled wilderness, to chase each other through the winter snow, and fetch balls and sticks in the riotous abundance of summer wildflowers. There is very little traffic on the rutted dirt roads, and consequently, bears, foxes, and even the occasional mountain lion sometimes lope across the streets. Perhaps you're already thinking, *What can she possibly know about inner peace in a busy world?*

For starters, I travel about 150 days a year. Peace can evaporate quickly on airplanes, in traffic jams, in seminars, in lonely hotel rooms, and when my computer turns demonic and digests the e-mail with a burp of satisfaction. Then there are our six adult children. I am the "not-so-evil-stepmother" of two remarkable young women and two fine young men; the grandmother of strapping, eight-year old Alex; and the mother of two wonderful sons. They keep me busy.

On my way up the mountain, I earned a Ph.D. in medical sciences from the Harvard Medical School, where I also completed three postdoctoral fellowships. A licensed clinical psychologist, I co-founded one of the country's first mind/body clinics in the early 1980s; did cancer research; and investigated the effect of emotions on immunity, health, and disease. I've been an assistant professor of anatomy and cellular biology at Tufts Medical School, and an instructor in medicine at the

Harvard Medical School. I spent several years in private practice as a psychologist; taught yoga and meditation; wrote ten books; created a large series of audiocassette tapes on health, healing, and spiritual growth; grew a business; and have an active career as a consultant and international speaker. Just writing about it makes me want to take a nap.

I won't pretend that juggling motherhood, marriage, and career has been easy. It has not. But a bout of serious stress-related illnesses, which descended like a flock of vultures when I was still in graduate school, taught me lessons about inner peace that made the following years much easier and more rewarding. Barely 25, I was tormented by migraine headaches, irritable bowel syndrome, and an immune disorder that led to frequent episodes of bronchitis and pneumonia. Within six months of learning some simple skills to manage my mind and taking up yoga to relax my body, the illnesses abated. I became a staunch believer in the mind/body effect.

In the 30 years that have passed since that time, the world has become progressively busier and more complicated. Telemarketers, arguably the devil's own spawn, reliably call during dinner. More television programs seem to exist than eyeballs to watch them. The Internet, with all its wonders, swallows some people whole. There are even support groups for computer junkies. And in a time when the media fosters the impression that every person needs an expensive car, electronic toys, and fancy restaurant meals, too many Americans are accumulating crippling debt. The average college undergraduate carries $2,748 in credit-card obligations. Thirty-two percent of these young people have four or more credit cards. They are going to be even busier than their parents were at the same age, just struggling to make the payments.

Comedian George Carlin quipped that he went into a bookstore and asked the clerk where the self-help section was. She refused to tell him since that would defeat the purpose. He could probably have followed the scuffs on the floor. In the year 2000, Americans spent $563 million on self-help books. It's little wonder. Approximately one in three people is sleep deprived, complaining of exhaustion and trouble holding things together. We are an anxious and worried culture. Between 1990 and 1997, the number of doctors' office visits for anxiety increased by 31 percent. The visits for panic disorder more than doubled. Approximately 12 percent of Americans are depressed, and another 10.2 percent have chronic "low mood." Seventy to 90 percent of visits to primary-care physicians are attributed to stress. And many more people suffer outside doctors' offices where the statistics are gathered. But *you* don't have to be a statistic.

Every day brings a choice: to practice stress or to practice peace. Finding inner peace doesn't require hours of daily practice. You don't have to stand on your head or stare at your navel. All it takes is a little willingness and common sense. Life is a precious gift to be savored, not an endless series of chores to complete while you complain about being "crazy busy." Remember—your to-do list is immortal. It will live on long after you're dead.

The 52 lessons in this book are simple steps that anyone can take to live in the present with more joy, courage, kindness, wisdom, and peace. The best way to use this book is to read it all the way through, getting a feel for the overall message. Then you can go back and put each chapter into action, one week at a time. Change is much easier and more exciting when you share your intentions and progress with someone you care about. Try reading a chapter to a friend, your mate, or an older child, and then discuss it together. Or form an Inner Peace Group and use the book as your springboard to action. Check in with each other on your progress. The process will bring you closer, and create a space where love and understanding can flourish. If you apply yourself to the simple lessons, the changes that take place are likely to be far more radical than you can begin to imagine.

As the Dalai Lama frequently reminds people, we are all alike in that our primary goal is the desire to be happy and to avoid suffering. The entire field of self-help, in all its aspects, is aimed at this very goal. As Albert Einstein once said of life, "It's simple, but not easy." My hope is that through the combination of science, story, psychology, and wisdom from the world's great spiritual traditions compiled in these pages, I have taken the simple . . . and made it easy. The rest is up to you.

∽ ∽ ∽

PART I

The Absolute
Basic Strategies
for Life

1. Relax and Be More Productive

When I was directing the Mind/Body Clinical Programs, a stress-disorders program at what is now the Beth Israel Deaconess Medical Center in Boston, many of the participants were high-powered executives. A little brush with a heart attack or cancer had them knocking reluctantly on my door. They wanted to use the power of their mind to heal, but were afraid that learning to relax would take away their competitive edge and dull their motivation. Visions of transcendental zombiehood danced through many minds. Some feared that they would have to trade their three-piece suits for a turban, and a lifetime of navel-gazing and herbal teas. More than once I heard the sentiment that it might be better to forget the whole thing and just die in the saddle.

My department chief and mentor, cardiologist Herbert Benson, M.D., knew better. In the late 1970s, he wrote an article for the *Harvard Business Review* featuring an arcane, but immediately obvious, relationship called the Yerkes-Dodson Law. Don't let the words scare you. Named after two intrepid physiologists, this handy little law looks like an upside-down letter U on a piece of graph paper. As stress increases (the x axis), so does productivity (the y axis). In other words, the more stressed you are, the better your output until you get to the top of the curve, where the upside-down U is poised to start down again. From there, it's a rapid downhill slide to poor productivity. Whereas mild to moderate stress helps us power through to-do's, more serious stress gives rise to the *un*-do's.

Let me give you a down-home case in point. If company is coming in an hour and the house is messy, I feel slightly stressed, and challenged to clean up so as to avoid looking like a slob. I get a certain look in my eye, and swoop into action like the white tornado. My husband, Kurt, calls this "getting initialized." My output is truly unbelievable. Like a thousand-armed goddess, I vanquish the dirt and sort the piles of clutter. But suppose, on a particularly bad dirt day, I find out that company is coming in ten minutes. The stress is so great, and the job seems so big, that I'm likely to get flustered and confused. I may then be found wandering around the house, looking dazed, with the same pile in my hand for several minutes. My internal wiring is sizzling, and smoke seems to be coming from my ears, because the load on the circuits is too large.

I believe that most busy, highly productive people operate in the high-stress range, somewhere on the descending limb of the stress/productivity curve. Their output is still high, but the internal wires are starting to short-circuit and burn. If they learned to relax and shifted back to the left on the Yerkes-Dodson curve, they would find themselves nearer to the top of the inverted *U*. Their output would actually be greater, while the toll on their body would be lessened. If they relaxed even more—to a point where it seemed like the turban was only another breath away—they would still be able to maintain the same output they had before, when they were burning out.

The only workable strategy for maintaining productivity over the long haul is to learn how to relax. There are literally thousands of ways to do that. My hope is that this book will give you suggestions that appeal to your unique physiology and preferences. I don't know what relaxes you, and neither does anyone else. You are the best and only judge of what it is that shuts off the internal dialogue that's always urging you to do more, do faster, and do better. But shut off the internal dialogue we must, if the clever system of body and mind is to restore itself and be available in its full power.

This week, put aside an hour a day—yes, I really mean that—to relax in whatever way you enjoy. You'll find that instead of constricting the amount of time available for you to get things done, the day will seem to unfold in a more languorous, spacious way. The to-do list will still get done, but you will live to tell about it.

2. Remember That Peace Is Already Within You

ॐ

When my grandson, Alex, was a toddler, he used to run around giggling at what seemed to be empty space. Sometimes his body would actually shake with excitement, and his face would light up for no apparent reason. His mother, Natalia, called this delightful behavior "talking to the angels."

That pure joy of playing in the mud, splashing in the tub, or playing peek-a-boo is innate. That inner radiance of peace and joy is our birthright, our own true nature. And while small children are effortlessly spontaneous and joyful, as adults we have to read books and go to classes to learn how to come back home to ourselves.

It's frustrating to believe that peace is some distant goal, attainable only by a few fortunate souls blessed with good genes, superior brain chemistry, plenty of money, or a calling as a monk. But peace has not deserted even the crankiest and busiest among us. The most basic fact about being human is that peace is our own true nature, our fundamental state of mind. There's a Buddhist saying that peace is like a sun that's always shining in your heart. It's just hidden behind clouds of fear, doubt, worry, and desire that continually orient you toward the past or the future. The sun comes out only when you're in the present moment.

I can still remember my first yoga class, adrenaline junkie that I am. After an hour of contorting like a pretzel, huffing and puffing, I'd forgotten everything but the sensations in my muscles. It felt great to give my busy brain a rest. It was time for the final relaxation pose, where you lie on your back and try to emulate a corpse. This is supposed to bring you back to your own true nature of peace. Everything slows down. Breathing practically stops as your muscles unwind and your mind goes into low gear.

The teacher walked among us and tested our level of relaxation by lifting an arm and letting it drop back to the floor. There were thuds all around. That got me thinking: *Everyone else is relaxed. That woman beside me hasn't breathed for a minute; she's practically a corpse. I always tense up under pressure. How can I let go when the teacher comes over and tests me?*

Before I realized what had happened, my arm had been lifted. It stayed up in the air like the leg of a dead canary. In spite of myself, I burst out laughing. Some yogi. But failure can be freeing, since there's nothing else to lose. After the laughter, I just let go. My limbs felt like they would have migrated to China if the floor hadn't been there. Exquisite feelings of peace flowed through me.

My God, I remember thinking, *this must be what people are talking about when they say that they're relaxed.* I hadn't felt that sensation since I was about Alex's age, when I sat in my father's lap and leaned my head on his chest while he told me stories.

As an adult, do you ever feel that you're "right here, right now"?

When you're in the present moment, past and future fade away. There are no mental conditions for happiness. The simple pleasures of a sunrise or a sunset, the breeze on your face, a smile that seems to reach into every cell of your body, or a heartfelt conversation are always available. When you're able to let go of thinking and relax, the clouds part. You automatically become like a child again and feel the radiant joy of the inner sun. When that sun shines, you feel whole—a part of something that extends far beyond your separate self.

The words *whole, holy,* and *healing* stem from the same root. In the holy moments of presence, you feel a kind of solidarity with life that is the very essence of inner peace. The problem is that most adults are rarely present. As the old saying goes, "The lights are on, but nobody's home." We seem to be awake, up and about, but life is passing us by while we're thinking about something else.

A lot of the exhaustion and world-weariness that we blame on being busy isn't from busyness at all. It's from being anywhere but in the present, laying down conditions for when we'll finally be able to come back home to ourselves. "When I make those phone calls, when my computer stops dumping my files, when I get a new car, when the kids go to bed, when my lover or spouse or boss finally appreciates me . . . then I can be happy." This would be like a five-year-old thinking, *When I'm a grown-up, then I'll be happy.*

Think about it. If not now, when? When you're dead?

Michelangelo was once asked how he was able to create such beautiful sculptures. He replied that he just chipped away the part of the stone that wasn't the sculpture. So it is with inner peace. The sculpture, the work of art, is already within you. Sculpting your life to reveal its essential beauty requires a consistent intention to chip away the insidious habits of mind that rob you of the childlike ability to stay present to the flow.

When you feel "crazy busy," try taking a breath, and let go of whatever is on your mind. Think, *Here I am.* Let your body relax, and feel your connection to the larger whole. This is not an easy task, but it becomes more and more possible with practice. Here you are. The possibilities for joy are all around you.

3. Save Your Breath and Keep Your Sanity

❧❧

Breathing is the single most important skill for calming body and mind. You may have noticed that as soon as you start feeling overwhelmed or anxious, your breath gets fast and shallow. You probably hold your breath intermittently as well so that its flow is ragged and irregular. Busy, stressed breathing accelerates your heart rate and signals your body to create anxiety-producing chemicals. This ancient mind/body feedback loop alerts you to danger, tenses your muscles in preparation for the kill or the great escape, and narrows your thinking. Such an automatic overdrive system comes in handy if you're fleeing from a mugger, but it's like stepping on the gas with your foot on the brake when the threat is no more serious than your to-do list. After a while, you burn yourself out.

Breathing is the only autonomic (meaning automatic—like heart rate, blood pressure, and body temperature) function over which we also have conscious control. While most people can't lower their heart rate or increase their body temperature at will unless they're trained in biofeedback, martial arts, or yoga, anyone can change their breathing. Breath is the link between body and mind, the royal road to calming down and returning your body to balance. Physiologists call this state *homeostasis*. All the body's systems are cooperating in perfect harmony.

If you practice martial arts, the "zen" of sports, you might call this state "being centered." The psychologist Mihaly Csikszentmihalyi, in his fine book, *Flow: The Psychology of Optimal Experience*, refers to it as "the flow state." It's where we do our best work, play our finest game, and experience creative thoughts and ideas bubbling up from a seemingly inexhaustible well. We are in our best self and feel a solid connection to the wholeness of life. This is the peaceful center, present inside you at all times. Proper breathing is the simplest way to access it. Since the only time that it's inappropriate to breathe is while you're underwater or caught in a poison gas attack, the practice of centered breathing is always available to you. Since you have to breathe anyway, it doesn't even take any extra time.

When you're in your center, you breathe like a baby. Watch an infant resting on its back, and you can observe that its belly swells like a balloon on the in-breath, and deflates on the out-breath. The rhythm is steady.

Take a moment right now and pay attention to your own breathing. Does your belly swell on the in-breath and relax when you breathe out, or does your chest rise and fall instead? Does your breath flow in a steady rhythm, or is it choppy?

Many adults can't feel their belly moving. Instead, their chest rises and falls while the abdomen stays rigid. It may even seem like your breathing is backward, and the belly flattens as you breathe in, rather than expanding. That's what happens when you use your chest muscles to expand the lungs rather than the diaphragm muscle. Using the chest muscles is tiresome. They can't inflate the lungs as well as the diaphragm, and you take in less oxygen than your hungry brain needs for sane thinking—so you breathe faster to compensate. Heart rate and blood pressure rise—and bingo! You're anxious, tired, and stressed.

The diaphragm is a large sheet of muscle stretched like a piece of thin rubber between the abdominal cavity and the lungs. It's shaped like an upside-down bowl. When it contracts on your in-breath, it flattens and pushes down on the organs in the abdominal cavity. Your belly expands. The negative pressure it creates in your lungs draws in air. When it relaxes and pops back up, the used air is pushed out of your lungs. Since the diaphragm is no longer putting pressure on the abdominal organs, your belly relaxes.

Shifting from stressed chest breathing to relaxed belly breathing is simple. Your body does it naturally every time you sigh or yawn. Why don't you give this breath-shifting exercise a try: Recline a little (lying down is even better), and place your hands flat on your belly to help you notice what's happening. Now take in a big breath and let it go with an audible sigh of relief. Breathe out as much air as you can. This resets the diaphragm. On the next in-breath, either feel or imagine that your belly is expanding. Feel or imagine it relaxing as you breathe out. Now take ten more belly breaths. If you like, you can count each breath, or even repeat the word *relax* or *centered* as you breathe out. Pay attention to what you feel.

Most often, people notice that their breathing rate slows way down and that they feel relaxed and centered. But for some people, there's an initial period of tension. After all, you're used to breathing without having to think about it. If you have asthma or other breathing difficulties, it's natural to feel a little strange at first, since breathing has anxious mental associations. This will pass sooner or later, usually with just a day or two of practice.

Belly breathing isn't brain surgery. Many people have heard of it. The problem is that most of us still don't do it. So, make a few *Save Your Breath* signs on note cards and post them where you'll see them. This week, make it a habit of checking on your breathing often, particularly when you feel rushed or overwhelmed. Give a sigh of relief, and concentrate on five or ten belly breaths. Think of this as feeling the way to your "sane center." Over time, that feeling will become familiar, like home. You will find it easier and easier to experience peace.

4. Build Your Brain Power

Someone sent me a note card with the saying, "The busier I am, the behinder I get." This is true as much for the brain as it is for the to-do list. When you neglect the basics of life, such as eating a good meal, taking a brisk walk, getting touched enough, or spending time in meaningful conversation, your brain chemistry suffers. When the brain is trying to operate on too few cylinders, it's hard to enjoy life or control your thinking. Instead, in spite of your best efforts, your thoughts are likely to control *you*.

An important skill for inner peace is to use your common sense to build a better brain. For example, pessimists are far more troubled by busy schedules than optimists are. They tend to be negative, rigid, and moody, paralyzing themselves with constant obsessing: "I'll never get this done. If I do, it won't be any good anyway. Then I'll get fired and my children will starve."

It's certainly possible to work with your thoughts to stop unproductive negative thinking, as we will do later in the book, but you also need to work with your brain. The part of the brain called the *deep limbic system*, a walnut-sized structure buried in the center, is responsible for a host of survival functions, including the way that you interpret the world emotionally. Is a given event positive, negative, or neutral? If your boss rushes by without saying hello, do you think that she hates you—and do you begin to obsess about it—or do you assume that she might just be preoccupied? Sophisticated brain scans indicate that when the deep limbic area is overactive, you're more likely to attach dire interpretations to her behavior.

An overactive limbic brain also saps motivation and will. It creates depression and makes it hard to get anything done.

But when the deep limbic area is quiet, the rose-colored glasses come out. You feel energetic and bright. The world is your oyster. You just love being busy and productive. When the boss rushes by without a glance, you think nothing of it. With a balanced limbic brain, you don't take things personally and store up hurt feelings.

You can learn the fine points of managing your brain chemistry by reading psychiatrist Daniel Amen's excellent book *Change Your Brain, Change Your Life*. He makes a very important point about overcoming negativity by engaging in simple behaviors that raise levels of the neurotransmitter, or brain hormone, *serotonin*.

One of the functions of serotonin is to quiet down the deep limbic brain, helping to eliminate worrying and obsessing. That's how Prozac works. But while antidepressant medications are a godsend for the truly depressed, most of us don't need medication to survive in a busy world. We just need common sense. What would your grandmother have told you? Eat a good meal, sit down and talk a while, give someone a hug, take a brisk walk outside, and stop to smell the roses. Do what makes you feel peaceful and relaxed. Dr. Amen might tell you exactly the same thing, except that you would be more likely to believe him since he's got the data to prove it.

Making enough serotonin to keep the limbic brain pacified requires protein, carbohydrates, and—thank God!—fat. Two studies have concluded that men with the lowest cholesterol levels had the highest suicide rates. Speaking from personal experience, I would hazard a guess that women on such diets tend more toward the homicidal. So what do you think happens if you decide to add some unbalanced fad diet like the all-hazelnut, all-gizzard, or all-bean sprout regimen to your busy life? You may lose a little weight in the short run, but you may also lose your peace of mind. Eating well-balanced meals and exercising may not seem too sexy or exciting, but it's the only method for weight loss that works in the long run, and that keeps your body and brain functioning smoothly.

If you're too busy to exercise, your brain as well as your muscles will suffer. Exercise increases brain uptake of the amino acid tryptophan, a precursor or building block of serotonin. Furthermore, exercise energizes. I always write better if I take a brisk walk first. Exercise increases metabolism, depresses the appetite, and helps keep weight regulated.

Grandma and Dr. Amen agree that touch is practically a panacea for our ills. It releases a growth hormone that helps the body restore itself, stimulates immune function, helps normalize heart rate and blood pressure, relieves pain, and stabilizes mood. It makes us feel happy and peaceful. Do we really need to spend millions of dollars on research before we pay attention to the obvious? The busier we've gotten, and the less common sense we've applied to basics such as eating, sleeping, exercise, communication, and touch, the more starved our brains have become.

This week, use your common sense. Eat delicious, but reasonable, meals. Chances are that you already know enough about nutrition—for example, fresh foods are better than processed; you can enjoy a little fat without consuming a stick of butter, and so on. Eating should be a pleasure, not a chemistry lesson. Exercise outdoors, even if all you can manage are a few good laps around the block every day. Sunshine is good for your pineal gland. It helps you release melatonin and sleep better. Ask for hugs. Give and receive a few back rubs. Spend some time in meaningful conversation. And stop to smell the roses, the coffee, the musk of a lover, or any other pleasing scent. The nerves from the nose feed directly into the limbic brain. Delicious aromas are potent stabilizers of mood.

5. Live with Passion

The happiest and most productive people are passionate about life. They radiate an infectious enthusiasm that makes "busyness" a pleasure rather than a problem. If you think back to a time when you felt passionate, you can probably still feel the sense of adventure and aliveness. If you were paying attention, you might also remember remarkable synchronicities that helped you along your way. I like to think of them as God's matching grants of grace.

This type of grant is how passionately busy people seem to perform feats bordering on the impossible, while keeping sane and centered. I used to feel that way about being a scientist. Hot on the tail of a discovery, I had the single-mindedness of a bloodhound on a scent. Staying in the lab until midnight wasn't a burden; it was a joy. I was turbo-charged with excitement that heightened my senses, ignited my intuition, and made me feel exquisitely grateful for life.

My scientific research was funded by the National Cancer Institute. Whenever a grant renewal was due, it seemed to rain miracles. The mail was often like a treasure trove. Dependably, colleagues would send papers that suddenly made my data fall into place, yielding unexpected insights. A trip to the medical library would turn up a review article with just the right information to support my theories and conclusions. A successful grant proposal would practically write itself.

A laser is a good analogy for the state of highly focused attention that courts success. Lasers are coherent beams of light in which all the particles are aligned, rather than scattered randomly. That alignment gives light the ability to cut through steel. Passion focuses your personal energy like a laser. Your coherent field of energy then brings other forces into alignment with it, just the way that a large grandfather clock, hanging on the wall with a group of other clocks, will entrain the other clocks' rhythms to its own. In a short period, the whole wall of clocks will have an identical "tick-tock" beat.

Without purpose, energy tends to remain scattered. It takes much more effort to manage even the mundane details of life, let alone create a masterpiece. Whether your passion is raising a family, redecorating a room, curing cancer, solving a mathematical theorem, cleaning your closets, building a deck, or surrendering yourself totally to any dream, passion brings together a confluence of unexpected opportunities that I think of as *grace*.

Now here's the paradox. When you're the kind of busy that's scattered and lacking in passion, it's hard to achieve a laserlike focus. Your days can become a burdensome exercise in simply getting things done, slogging through a swamp of responsibilities. The resultant fatigue and irritability cloud your vision. A low-level depression sets in that can be hard to overcome. It's a little bit like living underwater. If only you could break through the surface, a more exciting world would be clearly visible. But breaking the surface requires rest and respite. That's why a weekly Sabbath and daily periods of rest, contemplation, meditation, play, and reflection are so important. They allow you to get your head above water so that you can find your focus.

Periods of letting go are also critical to the creative process. The history of invention and discovery is filled with stories of people who work with enthusiasm, but can't quite break through to the "Aha!" The answer usually comes when they stop thinking and striving. The French mathematician Poincaré had one of the biggest mathematical "Ahas" of his career while stepping off a bus in the countryside on vacation. The chemist Kekulé discovered the circular structure of the benzene ring by dreaming of a snake with its tail in its mouth. And Einstein had his greatest "Aha" (related to his Theory of Relativity) while sailing on a boat one weekend—after spending many fruitless weeks laboring in his study.

There is an insidious idea in our culture that we alone are the "doer." This philosophy assumes that all ideas and actions spring from our isolated self. It tells us to set goals and work hard to achieve them. But these ideas are only partial truths. Every person is born with unique gifts to offer to the family of humanity. You know you're using them when excitement and passion fill you with joy and purpose. That's when unseen forces of evolution and coherence conspire to help you—opening up avenues that you might never have discovered alone.

This week, think about what ignites your passion. Reflect on those times that you've burned the brightest—busy and excited, yet peaceful and harmonious. Are you living your passion now? Are you taking the pauses that favor creativity? It's my hope that some of the entries that follow will help you.

In the meantime, you don't have to start by looking for your Purpose with a capital *P*. Try immersing yourself in a *small* passion. Perhaps there's a room you want to paint, a sweater to knit, or a garden to plant that excites you. Give yourself to the process. Like attracts like, and as your passion for the small things builds, life will fill you up more abundantly.

6. Practice Patience

🖝🖝

Busy people who pay attention to the many cues for success that life offers . . . stay on track. Their ability to focus makes them mindful of the world around them. This quality, which is sometimes known as patience, opens up a whole new universe of joy, peace, and possibility.

"James" was a friend of mine who died of AIDS in the late

1980s. He was a master of the art of patience. Before the advent of the new drug cocktails that can greatly prolong life, James was classified as a "long survivor." He had lived for seven or eight years with HIV, most of them symptom free. In that time, he had witnessed the deaths of many good friends. AIDS was truly like a plague back in those days, so his good health was a special blessing. He never took it for granted, and that made life sweet.

James was a grateful person, but beyond that, he was patient. One day I was watering his plants. Having a green thumb, this was a very pleasant task, as I got to know each plant individually. I turned some of them toward the light and wiped off their leaves. One of the plants was a large Christmas cactus, and most of the blooms were spent. As they fade, first the blossoms close, and then they hang there, all limp and droopy. After a few days, they get as dry as ancient rice paper and finally fall off. If you have a large Christmas cactus, like James did, the falling blossoms make a big mess. Thinking I'd spare him the effort of crawling around on his hands and knees and picking up the debris, I began to pinch off the dying blooms.

James put his hand gently on my arm. "Joanie," he said, "everything has a life and a destiny. People, trees, plants, clothes, even stones. And the cycle isn't done for these flowers yet. I know they're kind of ratty looking and that they've passed their peak. But please, let them finish life on their own timetable. I'm happy to pick them up off the floor."

I watched the blooms fall over the next few days. Indeed, there was a special beauty in their final transformation from living tissue to fragile, papery phantoms. There was a profound rightness about the moment when they let go and fluttered down. I picked up the papery husks and lay them outside under a hedge, where they could go back to the earth again. Instead of viewing the dying blossoms as a mess-in-the-making,

James had helped me see more deeply and patiently into their essence.

I am not a generally patient person. It's a practice that takes constant awareness. Even after James's lesson in letting life unfold through its full cycle, sometimes I still want to pull off the dead blooms, rush people in conversation, curse at the traffic, and hurry through a fine meal.

I once heard *patience* defined as "impatience stretched to its limit." The implication was that most people have no idea what patience really is. In the name of patience, we often hold back like a pit bull straining against its leash. We are not present at all—just trying to look pleasant while our blood boils. Inside, we're wishing that the traffic would clear, that our child would go to bed, or that our colleague would shut up already. A lot of energy is used up in the name of this false patience.

Real patience requires a gentle willingness to let life unfold at its own pace. This willingness, in turn, requires mindfulness. If I'm present to the fading blossoms as they are, there's a subtle beauty in their dying that is no less engaging than in their opening. The beauty is not so much in the flower as in the relationship to it. That which we have truly known and loved in all its phases is more precious still as it fades away. The same was true of James. He was as beautiful in his dying as he was at the height of his power. In the years since his death, I have acquired three large Christmas cactuses. When their brief and prolific blooming comes to an end, I think of James and send him a blessing.

Patience is an opportunity to love deeply, and to wring the last drop of juice out of life. This week, notice the times that you're impatient. What's the hurry? Think about what you'll lose by rushing the blossom in its leave-taking, or hurrying your loved one in conversation. What will you gain by leaping out of the tub two minutes faster, rather than savoring the way your muscles start to relax? Identify one area where you tend to lose patience, and try giving it full, mindful attention.

Patience is peace. Learning to be patient is a continual practice that takes years to ripen. Let it unfold, day by day, and be gentle with yourself in the learning.

෴ ෴ ෴

PART II

Strategies for
Taking Care
of Yourself

7. Be a Better Juggler

I was about to give a talk to a society of businesswomen in Atlanta one winter. One of the organizers took me by the hand and made a heartfelt plea: "Please don't talk to us about living in balance. No one does. Even airplanes veer off course during the trip, and they have computers to guide them. Just teach us how to be better jugglers."

She had a good point. One of the ubiquitous polls on how Americans live revealed that a mere 2 percent of us believe that our lives are in balance. The problem is not so much that they *aren't*, as much as that we think they *should* be. The belief that there's a way to organize our time so that everything stays in balance can lead to the conclusion that there's something desperately wrong with our unbalanced ways. Perhaps a more livable truth is that we're jugglers rather than tightrope artists. From that perspective, we can accept that some things will always be up in the air. Outer balance isn't always possible. The trick is to keep our eye on the balls, and to manage their perpetual flight with grace and *inner* balance.

Juggling is a familiar metaphor. The late Yale psychologist and author Daniel Levinson, who wrote about the passages in men's and women's lives, interviewed people at different segments in the life cycle. Many of the 40-something women who both worked and had children commented on the disheartening myth of the Superwoman. By 40, you realize that there *is* no Superwoman, they concluded irritably. Who can keep all the demands of life in balance? The best you can do is keep juggling. Almost all of the women planned to do more for themselves in the second half of life than they had in the first. The mistake that many of us make, I think, is waiting until we're 40 to voice that intention.

Juggling requires maintaining your center. The idea is to stop managing life so much, and begin managing yourself. Long ago I learned that it's better to prepare the speaker than the speech, particularly when I'm well acquainted with the subject matter. If I meticulously outline a lecture, rehearsing the points as I get ready to begin, I'm likely to lose my center. But if I chat with the audience first, put myself at ease, or take a few minutes for some deep breathing, the talk always goes more smoothly.

When I'm centered, it's easier to respond to people, to catch the nuances of their attention, and to let inspiration flow through me. Thinking of myself as an instrument that life plays, rather than the source of the melody, has helped me be a better juggler. The instrument needs to be cleaned and polished, treated with care. When I'm in balance, the unbalanced hodgepodge of things on the to-do list are accomplished more effectively.

After my speech in Atlanta, there was a panel discussion. Three women took us through their average work day. The youngest, single and without children, was already a busy professional with little time for herself. A 30-something mother of three, with an infant, a toddler, and a six-year-old, spoke next. Her career was even more demanding than that of the younger woman, but with the help of her husband and a nanny, she kept her balls in the air with a lot of humor and a tremendous zest for life. The third panelist was a single mother of two. Aside from parenting and work, her biggest priority was her church, in which she was very active. Those activities rejuvenated her and gave her the inner strength to keep all the other balls in the air.

The youngest woman asked how she could cope with her perception that, single and childless, she should do more at work than colleagues with relationships or families. As a group, we concluded that you have to honor your priorities at every stage of life. If going to choir practice or a yoga class keeps you happy, why is it any less important than getting home to be with your family? "Learn to set boundaries," the other women counseled her. "You have to realize that you're worth it. You're entitled to create a life for yourself."

We all have to carve out time for the meaningful things that help us stay centered. I've noticed the tendency in many people to cut out just those types of activities in the name of simplicity and balance. But if you don't take care of yourself, no one else will do it for you. Without boundaries, work will expand to take up as much time as you have. It's up to you to choose those things that keep you centered—even when they appear to make life busier.

This week, review your priorities. If self-care is not one of them, think of an activity that you would really enjoy and add it to your to-do list. This may seem like it will make you even busier, but the truth is that it will actually generate more productive time. Feeding your soul with the things you love creates happiness and gives you energy. Taking the time to enjoy life is one of the most important secrets of busy people with inner peace.

8. Honor the Precious Person Inside of You

☙☙

I learned this simple lesson in self-care from my friend Tina Lear, a talented musician who arrived a day late for an annual summer gathering of friends on beautiful Cortes Island in British Columbia. Old-growth forest, ocean waters, distant snow-capped peaks, and killer whales spouting as they swim the passageway to Alaska make Cortes a magical place. But getting to this idyllic paradise can be a major hassle. The island is remote, accessible only by seaplane, boat, or a chain of ferries. Tina was so busy launching a new CD that she almost didn't make the trip.

The night she arrived, about 30 of us were gathered up on a hill in a large white tent that serves as a meeting room. The evening activity was a storytelling circle. When it was your turn, you had three minutes to tell a story from your life, or from the life of a loved one or friend.

Tina, petite and pretty, strode quickly and purposefully to the center, with her hands on her hips, already getting into character as her hassled self the day before. She had been so busy that she had thought about staying home to work rather than joining us. Then she had a breakthrough. Tina saw herself "from the outside" and became a kind of witness to her dilemma. She did a fabulous rendition of scurrying around, trying to get everything done. Then she acted out the moment of awakening, the "Aha" when she understood how busyness can be a subtle form of violence.

"Would I be acting this way if Thich Nhat Hanh [a well-known Vietnamese Buddhist meditation teacher and peace worker] moved into me? If I were hosting him, like my body was a house?" she pondered aloud. Tina went through her whole inner dialogue. Would she really make that saintly old man give up lunch, even though he was hungry, just because she was too busy to stop? Would she forbid him to pee because it took up too much time? Would she call him names if he were slow, and demand that he move faster? When he needed a nice mindful walk, a time just to breathe and take in the fullness of summer's abundant beauty, would she keep him prisoner in her office until the last envelope was licked?

We all got the point, roaring with laughter. Why is any one of us less valuable than Thich Nhat Hanh, Albert Einstein, Mother Teresa, Jesus, the Buddha, the Beatles, the Dalai Lama, the Pope, our own beloved children, our aging parents, or our very best friend? We wouldn't even think of treating the people we love and respect the way we treat ourselves when we're possessed by busyness. In truth, most people wouldn't treat strangers—or perhaps even their worst enemies—with the kind of thoughtless cruelty they inflict so willingly upon themselves.

Think of a person whom you love and respect. For the next week, each time you forget how to care for yourself, pretend that someone dear and precious lives inside you. Honor that person, and treat them with all the respect they deserve. If you adopt this as a daily practice, little by little a strange and wonderful transformation will occur. You will remember how to be good to yourself. And you will experience how much more creative and productive you are when you know that you're worthy of your own care and love.

9. Keep Track of Your Energy Reserves

❧❧

One January I went to the Caribbean to teach a relaxing, week-long personal growth program. The waters were a superb shade of aquamarine. The sunsets were magnificent. And I was a crispy critter, exhausted and disheartened. I had traveled more than 200 days the previous year, with too little support on the work and home fronts. Then, over the Christmas holidays, a long-time employee had left under the most difficult circumstances. I had spent my precious time off fielding phone calls, getting my taxes ready, and finally hiring and training a new staff person. Busy to the max, I had failed to keep track of my energy reserves and found that the "well" had run dry.

One afternoon, my husband and I went for a sail with some of the people from the group. A vivacious redhead by the name of Donna and I got to talking. And as women often do, we went straight to the heart of the matter. A corporate trainer and coach, Donna was also used to a heavy travel schedule, but she'd learned to manage it. At one point, she leaned in close to me and took my hand. "Do you know that the life force is almost gone from your eyes?" she said. I could only nod affirmatively and sniffle a little. "Would you let me help you?" she asked.

"Dr. Donna," as she is known, became my friend, corporate consultant, and self-care coach.

One of the most important things she asked was elegant in its power and simplicity: "On a scale of 1 to 10, where 1 is empty and 10 is full, how full is your well?" I knew immediately what she meant. Was I joyful, creative, rejuvenated, and frisky, or was I despondent and dragged out?

I answered immediately, "I'm sucking mud." This, I knew from long training and experience as a mind/body medical researcher and psychologist, was dangerous ground. My immune system was at a low ebb, my muscles were achy, and I felt poised on the brink of physical disaster. I was a poor advertisement for mind/body health and centered living. By failing to pay attention to my energy reserves, I had let myself wander into hazardous territory.

The "well scale" gave me a handle for recovery and a way to stay honest about taking care of myself. Awareness is the prerequisite for change. Realizing that you're at the bottom is a wake-up call. You have two choices: to rise or to die. I decided on the former. I also committed to staying alert to my energy levels so that I wouldn't use up my reserves, run on empty, and risk either emotional or physical disaster again.

During the period of extreme stress that had led to sucking mud, I did exactly what most people do when their backs are against the wall. I regressed. Bounding out of bed to deal with the office meltdown, I neglected to eat until late afternoon. Then I grabbed anything that was convenient. As my sons say, I ate a balanced diet from the four food groups:

candy, cake, pies, and cookies. Nonetheless, I lost five pounds. This is called the high-stress diet. For a person who normally favors liberal quantities of fruit and vegetables, poor eating was a danger sign. I'd gone into survival mode. Exercise, which above all, fills my well, was a thing of the past. I couldn't tear myself away from the office. The only positive coping strategy that remained was the support of my husband and the love and counsel of good friends.

If I have a single favorite gripe with God, it's this: Good habits are so hard to form and sustain, while bad habits are a breeze. Most of us have times when we forget everything we know about taking care of ourselves, and then we have to pull ourselves up by the bootstraps.

So, reform was mandatory. I started exercising again and eating well. Several times a day, I would check the well scale, and once a week I'd report in to "Dr. Donna."

"Hey, I'm a 5, a 7, or even a 10." Over the next several months, it became clear that 7 was the cut-off point for feeling peaceful. Below that, anxiety and obsession kicked in, and creativity was hard to tap in to.

Fancy scales aren't required to measure your stress level, although many of them exist. The simplest way to find out how you're coping is to draw a horizontal line on a sheet of paper. Mark the far-left point "1," and the far-right "10." Then put a vertical line wherever you think it belongs to represent your stress level. Research shows that this simple measure is as good as the sophisticated scales. The well scale is really a vertical version of the same thing, but I think it's even more powerful because it's such an engaging and positive metaphor.

Your objective is to fill the well and stay aware of exactly where you are. When my well drops below 7, a mental alarm goes off. Energy reserves are getting low. I know that I need to do something rejuvenating or I'll start a downward slide. Restorative things fall into two categories: (1) things that you can do immediately—such as taking a walk, adjusting your breathing, doing some stretching, getting into a hot shower, having some fun, talking to a friend, cuddling up with your pet, and the like; and (2) developing long-range life strategies.

Some of the long-range strategies that worked for me revolved around two more scales. When deciding what jobs to take, they had to fall below a 7 on the schlep scale, a measure of wear and tear. Going to India is a 10. Having someone drive me the two hours from Boulder to Colorado Springs is a 1 on the schlep scale. So I learned to make less stressful choices.

Then there was the service scale. Did a particular job match my vision of service? Running a retreat for cancer patients was a 10; consulting on the development of graduate programs was a 1 on the scale. Developing my vision and realizing what my time was worth led to other changes. I hired more staff and put an end to driving home from the airport late at night, contributing to public safety as well as personal peace.

This week, start keeping track of your energy reserves. Try using the well scale. At least three times a day, determine how full your well is. What is the cut-off point when you start to lose steam and feel overwhelmed? Figure out what raises the water level for you quickly, and take action right away when you need to revive yourself. Taking a ten-minute walk instead of returning the next phone call can change the course of your entire day.

Once you have a handle on immediate ways to fill the well, you can begin thinking about long-term strategies. While many people can't afford to hire a coach, everyone can do a little reciprocal coaching with a buddy. My own good friend, Cheryl Richardson, has written two best-selling books that can get you started: *Take Time for Your Life* and *Life Makeovers*. Her on-line newsletter, which you can subscribe to at **www.cherylrichardson.com**, is also very valuable.

10. Choose Activities That Bring You to Life

One of the most common complaints I hear from busy people is that they feel squeezed out of their own lives. Their needs are the last to be met, and the very activities that make them feel joyful and alive seem beyond their grasp. There are simply too many other things to do. I must hear the self-help advice: "Secure your own oxygen mask first, before you help anyone requiring your assistance" at least twice a week. It's based on the actual announcement that flight attendants make before take-off, which I also hear about twice a week. And while the phrase is overused as analogies go, the reason for its popularity is that it hits the mark. If you're so busy trying to save the people around you that you black out, all of you are likely to die.

I gave years of lip service to this folk wisdom while earnestly ignoring it. Perhaps that's because most of us need to recognize a good idea and then think about it for a while before we actually implement it. The lag between knowing and doing isn't neurotic; it's normal. We're just gearing up for change.

But the other reason we shouldn't ignore the airplane advice is that doing without real oxygen has immediate and powerful negative consequences. Doing without *virtual* oxygen—the things that make you feel better in the long run—is much more abstract. For example, friends sustain me, but I won't expire immediately if I don't see them for a while. Touch sustains me, but I once lived quite happily in an ashram for three weeks without any touch at all (if you don't count the centipedes that crawled over me in bed at night). Exercise sustains me, but for a year after a car accident, during which I lived with post-concussion syndrome, I hardly exercised at all. I'm still here.

It's easy to delude ourselves with the notion that we will

always be here. We can take care of ourselves later. Right now our children, spouse, friends, or career need us more. People who actually have brushes with death and go through the equivalent state of permanently losing their oxygen, often make drastic changes in their priorities. Many speak of the renewed importance of the three *F*'s: faith, family, and friends—because that's where the love is. And in the end, love is what matters most. The reasons these people give for securing their own oxygen masks first is that doing so helps them feel more loving, patient, and kind. When they take the time for themselves, they can show up for their loved ones more willingly and authentically.

Securing your oxygen mask means different things to different people. Other than your work—even if you love it—what are the things that nourish you and bring out your best self? Take a few minutes this week and make an oxygen list.

In no particular order, mine would include playing golf, skiing, hiking, being with my grown children, intimate conversations with my husband, sex, prayer, mystery novels, inspiring movies, singing, sharing time with friends, massages, laughing, playing word games, romping with our four dogs (Mixer, Sasquatch, Gremlin, and The Squeezirat), sitting by a fire and listening to music, being outside and taking in the silence, dancing, craft projects, cooking for friends, horseback riding, hanging around in my bathrobe until lunchtime reading magazines and staring at the ceiling, yoga, exploring new places, long road trips, foreign cultures, and hot fudge sundaes.

I get to some of the things on the list pretty regularly, others hardly at all. Six months ago, I made a commitment to get a massage every week. It has increased my energy, reduced my stress, and made me feel ten years younger. This winter I'm making a commitment to ski at least six times. Last winter went by without a single outing. When you live in a world-class ski area, that's a shame.

So study your oxygen list and discuss it with a friend. Choose something that you'd like to make a more regular part of your life—and commit to doing it.

11. Ask for Help

Asking for help when you need it seems like a no-brainer. It's an obvious strategy for self-care. But can you let go of control long enough to actually receive the help you need? A lot of busy people can't. Their "damn-the-torpedoes-full-speed-ahead-I'm in-charge-here" operating style tends to stop would-be helpers in their unsuspecting tracks.

As an example, it was a busy day at the clinic many years ago. By mid-morning, we were all pooped, up to our ears in charts to fill out, research to write up, and patients to see. So I volunteered to make a run to the cafeteria for coffee. When I got into the elevator on the way back, both of my hands were full. Several other people also stepped in, and I had a fleeting thought of asking someone to push the button for our floor. But the moment of sanity passed, and I pushed the button with my nose. An elderly woman remarked, "Good God, my dear. You could have asked for help. That's an important thing, you know."

I was just starting to learn. Like many busy and efficient people, I liked doing things myself. It seemed easier than asking someone else. And if you do it yourself, you always know that the job will get done just the way you want. But an insidious problem takes root. Because you rarely ask for help, and often refuse it when it's offered, the people around you gradually stop asking. You get exactly what you asked for: the opportunity to work yourself to death. Inevitably, resentment builds up, as in: "Am I the only one who ever gets anything done around here?!"

A few years ago, I was giving a weekend workshop when I was gifted with another lesson on accepting help. On Saturday afternoon, the room we were using had to be cleared out for another program. I had a lot of supplies to pack and schlep up the long hill to my room. No problem. Busy people come well prepared, and I had brought along a suitcase on wheels. One of the attendees offered to help me clean up and cart away the supplies. I politely declined, stating the obvious: "Thanks, but I really don't need any help. I have a suitcase with wheels."

The woman stood there with her hands on her hips, shaking her head and tapping her foot. "Joan, you don't get it, do you? This isn't about wheels. It's about accepting help. And accepting help is about feeling like you're worth it. Which you are. Now get with the program."

We trudged up the hill together while I clenched my hands behind me to stop from grabbing the suitcase. It was clear that I had a serious control issue. To make matters worse, the Good Samaritan insisted on coming to my room the next morning so that she could wheel the suitcase back to our meeting room. Her parting words found their mark: "You speak so eloquently about kindness. Remember that letting people help you gives them an opportunity to be kind. Refusing help is a subtle kind of selfishness, you know." I wondered why that obvious fact had escaped me for so long.

Being a control freak extends beyond the inability to ask for help. For example, I have a friend who likes her bottles of vitamin pills lined up in a specific order. Her husband, who could not fathom this esoteric system, always messed up the order. They used to have fights about it. To keep the peace, the couple finally decided to buy two sets of vitamins, his and hers. Go figure. It's important to pick your battles wisely if you want a peaceful life. It's also important to maintain your perspective. Ask yourself how vital the order of the vitamins really is. Is it worth a fight?

Humorist and author Loretta LaRoche uses a set of props to demonstrate how different cognitive distortions drive us crazy. A Viking hat with horns represents the control freak. She suggests that if you have that tendency, you can buy yourself a similar hat and wear it when the mood strikes. For example, my friend could don the horns and swoop into the kitchen like a commanding general to confront her husband. "Get out of the way you slob, and let me show you how to organize those pills!"

Loretta's point is that the very idea of acting like a crazed conqueror is so funny—once you appreciate your bizarre behavior—that you may actually be able to stop before you give yourself a stroke. I wish I could say that my horns were in mothballs, but I still like to be in charge. Short of another hundred years in therapy, that's unlikely to change. But I *have* learned to take it lightly, bite my tongue upon occasion, choose my battles wisely, and ask for help even when it's a struggle.

This week, focus on giving and receiving help. If you have trouble asking for the assistance you need, then practice. It's easier than learning to play the piano. Three times a day, even if you have to invent a reason, ask someone to help you. Try asking for directions, even if you know the way. If they're lousy, you are doubly blessed. You might really have been lost, so you can be grateful that you know where you are. Plus, you've provided a stranger with an opportunity to be kind.

If you tend to expect too much from others, practice giving help. Three times a day this week, offer to be helpful without being asked. Open the door for someone. Bring a cup of coffee or a cold drink to a co-worker or a loved one. Ask the people around you if there's anything you can do for them. You'll be amazed by how much more receptive to your requests they'll be in the future.

12. Take a Sabbath

❦❦

My friend Wayne Muller is a therapist, minister, and founder of Bread for the Journey—a group of regionally based, grass-roots charitable organizations that give people seed money to begin self-sustaining projects in their communities. Author of the magnificent book *Sabbath*, Wayne reminds us that God didn't just *suggest* that we rest once in a while; it was a commandment right up there with do not steal or kill. Think about it. Why was rest important enough to be a commandment rather than just a good idea?

In the Judeo-Christian creation story, the world was made in six days. On the seventh day, God rested and enjoyed Creation. For observant Jews, the Sabbath is the holiest day of the year, even though it occurs 52 times annually. It affords a weekly opportunity to rest and be with loved ones, to rejuvenate for the week to come, to feel grateful, and to say of the fruits of our labors, "Hey, this is pretty good." Without the busyness of television, computers, errands, cooking, phone calls, faxes, e-mails, handling money, or doing work of any kind, there's nothing left to do but rest, celebrate, and make love. The latter is a Sabbath commandment for married Jews. I always thought that if this were widely known, there would be more converts.

This kind of Sabbath may seem like an extreme practice, and it is. Nevertheless, you might want to try it at least once. The idea is to abandon work altogether. Do all your cooking the day before, and leave the Sabbath plates to wash the next day. Even the dish police need a day off. Invite some friends to come by. Play music together, sing, or dance. Have intimate conversations about things of beauty and meaning. If you have small children, read to them and play games. A day off in our culture usually means time to do errands and catch up on non-work busyness. Sabbath is a day off from *all* busyness.

Taking a day of rest is so far removed from the way most of us live that Hollywood could practically make reality TV out of the concept. Will the Jones family survive the Sabbath? When I was a child growing up in Boston, we had the famous Blue Laws, which meant that stores were closed on Sunday. There was no hopping in the car to go to the supermarket or the mall. In fact, there *were* no malls. Fast food was still a gleam in the devil's eye.

Sunday was a family day when almost everybody gathered with their clan and had a leisurely time of it, eating and catching up on the events of the week. Our family usually gathered at my paternal grandparents' home. The little troop of cousins played together while the adults smoked, drank cocktails; and discussed politics, religion, and local happenings. Dinner was an event. We sat at a long table like something out of the movie *Tom Jones* and ate what we kids called "roast beast."

I know people who pride themselves on working seven days a week. They almost never take an hour—let alone a day—to rest. They have beautiful homes—and more to the point—beautiful families that they rarely take the time to appreciate. There are no rest stops to enjoy what has been created. Wayne Muller compares rest to the pauses in music that create rhythm. Without them, the beautiful arrangement of notes that make up music is merely noise. It's the pauses that birth melodies. It's rest that makes creation beautiful.

For years I thought about adopting a weekly Sabbath, but since the majority of my work is done on weekends, it isn't feasible. I might rest, but I might also starve. This is the line between work and rest that many of us walk. So, I went to see a wise and offbeat rabbi. His advice was to take the Sabbath I *could*, not the one that I *couldn't*. Four hours on a Wednesday afternoon might do for a start. The intention to rest—and a reasonable plan that could work—was more important than adhering to the letter of the law.

This week, plan at least a mini-Sabbath. Perhaps it will last only two or three hours. Maybe you'll get so excited by the idea that you'll take an entire day. Involve anyone you live with in the planning. Will you take a hike and go for a picnic together? If so, what will the menu be? Sitting on the grass together, under the shade of a tree, perhaps you'll think of a question that each person can answer, such as: "What are you grateful for?" or "What is your most cherished dream?" Listen carefully and drink deeply of one another and of life. That's what the commandment Thou Shalt Rest is all about.

13. Go Out into Nature

Over the years, I've informally polled thousands of people about the things they do to take care of themselves. Going out into nature is at the top of the list. Returning to the natural world is my favorite self-care activity as well, and has been since childhood.

At 16, when I finally had the driver's license that most teens covet, my first big excursion was a day's mini-wilderness trip. Two friends and I, eager to leave suburbia for something wilder and more primal, packed our knapsacks and set out for western Massachusetts. We hiked by a stream, entranced by the pink roots of willow trees that floated like fairy hair in the shallow water. Lying on our backs in a grassy field, faces warmed by the late autumn sun, we watched the patterns of the clouds. The sweet fragrance of hay rose from the earth to touch the sky.

Toward evening, we collected deadfall and kindled a fire over which we roasted hamburger shaped into long rolls around green sticks. We sang favorite songs and shared the stories of our lives around the flickering magic of the fire. As we gathered our things by the light of the moon, three very different girls from the ones who had left suburban Boston that morning piled back into the car. We smelled of wood smoke and grass . . . of contentment. Peace, I learned, has a scent all its own. In some indefinable way, we had come home to ourselves, entrained by the rhythm of the natural world.

As an adult who lives on the edge of the wilderness, surrounded by the majesty of purple mountain peaks and riots of wildflowers in their short season, I still have to make a concerted effort to enjoy nature. And I'm not alone. During a trip to Hawaii, I invited the woman who had brought me there to take a walk on the beach. She was a bit shocked. It had been years since she had left the harried routine of home and office to enjoy a walk along the ocean that lay like a shimmering jewel at her feet. The invitation to find peace was all around, but she was too busy to accept it.

We are part of the natural world, interdependent with it, even though our culture tends to isolate us from it. But we cannot exist in a healthy balance outside nature because our bodies evolved in concert with it. For example, we need the cues of daybreak and nightfall to regulate brain function, emotions, and physical maturation. Modern girls reach puberty significantly earlier than young women did a hundred years ago. This is due in part to electric lights that make days unnaturally long and nights too short. The great biologist René Dubos believed that as we are retreating further and further from nature, we're becoming mutants. The earth is not only our home; it's also a biological regulator. And it's available to every person, rich or poor, unless we're unfortunate enough to be in jail.

The best vacation in our family's memory was a camping trip we took when the children were small. We had very little money, so we rented a campsite on magnificent Martha's Vineyard and brought all our food, even the cans of lemonade that saved us from having to buy higher-priced sodas. We rode our bikes, went to the beach, and cooked simple dinners over an open fire. It was the happiest week we can remember. No hotel has nearly the amenities that nature does. It's worth a few bug bites, and even a mild case of poison ivy, to forage for wild berries or fish in a stream. Nature awakens deadened senses. It has the power to bring you back to life again.

This week, think about your relationship to the natural world. Make a plan with family or friends to spend a day hiking, fishing, snowshoeing, horseback riding, cross-country skiing, sitting by a lake or a stream, camping out in a tent under the stars, cooking over an open fire, or whatever you can all agree on.

Even on days when you have to be inside, take a few breaks to walk around the block or even to look out the window. One research study found that people whose hospital rooms overlooked nature healed faster than those whose view was of a parking lot.

So, if your window *does* overlook a parking lot, get a plant and put it on the sill. Tend it with care. Enjoy each new leaf as it unfolds. Nature can sustain you and bring you peace, even when it's working its magic from a pot.

14. Enjoy Music for Peace, Creativity, and Healing

Music is filled with memories. When my mother was dying, wondering whether my father would be there to greet her on the other side, my son Justin intuitively gave me the high sign and whispered "Some Enchanted Evening." Together, we softly sang the song that my parents had fallen in love to. Although we couldn't remember all the words, the melody was enough. My mother's face relaxed, and for just a moment, she looked like a young girl again, seeing her true love for the very first time.

Music is like a tuning fork for the brain. It can stimulate specific regions, soothing emotions, boosting the capacity for learning, and unlocking creative genius. It can also help the body to heal, reduce stress, and initiate sleep. Therese Schroeder-Sheker, who works at St. Patrick's Hospital in Missoula, Montana, is a pioneer in the use of music for the dying. She and the 20 interns whom she trains annually in her two-year certificate program maintain a vigil by patients' bedsides. There, they play plainchants (similar to Gregorian chants) on the harp and sing. Research indicates that patients' pain and anxiety are substantially reduced, and they receive the gift of inner peace in their passing.

Don Campbell, a concert pianist and master of the use of music in education, healing, and creativity, is a dear friend and author of the best-sellers *The Mozart Effect* and *The Mozart Effect for Children*. Pardon the pun, but his works have obviously struck a chord, since millions of the CDs and cassette tapes that accompany his books have also been sold. *Strengthen the Mind* features music for intelligence and learning, *Heal the Body* presents music for rest and relaxation, and *Unlock the Creative Spirit* focuses on music for imagination and creativity. Don chose other musical selections especially for the needs of pregnant mothers, infants, and children.

The director of the coronary-care unit at Baltimore Hospital states that listening to classical music for half an hour produces the same effect as ten milligrams of Valium. Don Campbell cites research showing that music can help alleviate conditions ranging from migraine headaches to attention deficit disorder and substance abuse. A study done at the University of California at Irvine showed that spatial intelligence, an important component of IQ, was boosted significantly when students listened to just ten minutes of classical music before they were tested. PET scans of the working brain reveal the power of music to shift neural processing. High-frequency melodies, like those of Mozart, for example, help stimulate the language centers of the brain.

Unfortunately, some people hold strong negative judgments about classical music. They think of it as boring, snobbish, highbrow, or inaccessible. But if you take the time to really listen, you will discover why it has endured through the centuries. And the great musical masters are far more human than some people think. Remember the movie *Amadeus?* Mozart was no dusty fossil. He was called the "Eternal Child"— an eccentric, joyful genius filled with naiveté and hope. His pure and inspired music is a direct route to your inner essence of peace, creativity, and wisdom.

The music of the great masters, including Beethoven, Bach, Albinoni, Telemann, Scarlotti, Mozart, Vaughan Williams, Handel, and Chopin, are a balm for my soul. Like many people, I'm captivated by Pachelbel's *Kanon,* which can free blocked emotions and restore inner peace. If I need courage to act, or have lost inspiration, Mussorgsky's *Pictures at an Exhibition*, particularly the movement called "The Great Gate of Kiev," can infuse new purpose and creativity into my life. Music truly has the power to bring us home to ourselves.

I'm thrilled that Don Campbell offered to collaborate with me to produce a special volume of classical music, *Inner Peace for Busy People: Music to Relax and Renew,* to go with this book. We hope that it will give you as much peace and joy as it gave us during its production. You can find ordering information for the CD in the "Inner Peace Kit" section at the back of the book. I've also included the script for *A Musical Journey for Busy People*, to be used with the CD, in this resource section.

This week, explore the power of classical music to relax, heal, inspire, and restore you. If you have your own collection, you may already be using it for your self-care. If not, classical music is as close as your radio or local library. Try a little Mozart or Bach. Give yourself to the music mindfully, and notice the effects that different pieces have on you. You will have discovered one of the world's most enduring treasures.

15. Make the Mundane Sacred

❦❦

I took a trip to Bali several years ago. This small island, surrounded by a turquoise sea, is the most peaceful place I've ever visited. There are temples to four of the Hindu gods arranged at the cardinal points of the island, and a Mother Temple sits atop a hill in the center. The temples are like guardian spirits keeping the land and her people in balance. Everywhere you look, from sun umbrellas to seat covers, black-and-white checkered cloth is evident. It represents the equilibrium between good and evil and reminds people that their personal choices affect the harmony of the universe. In Bali, even mundane things are reminders of the sacred.

Each lot of land is laid out in a prescribed manner. There's a special area for the garden; for the dwelling; and for the ornate, steepled temple where the occupants of the home leave food offerings for the gods. Artistically arranged baskets of fruit, flowers, and incense are set outside each workplace in the morning. Harmony reigns even during the routine of doing business. People continually remember their place in the family of things. The entire manner in which the Balinese live is in the spirit of nurturing and self-care.

The Balinese are a peaceful, creative people. They craft intricate wood carvings, magnificent paintings, and every type of art imaginable. Even the rice paddies, laid out in jeweled squares, are like reflections of a divine being. Beautiful rockwork, gurgling fountains, and still pools overflowing with an abundance of lotus flowers are commonplace. It's a land as close to a Garden of Eden as the human heart and mind can fathom. When national television begins its daily broadcast, the haunting melody of the "Gayatri Mantra," a prayer of peace and gratitude, issues from each set, once again proclaiming the union of the mundane and the sacred. Daily life in Bali is worship in its purest form.

In Western culture, we tend to separate the sacred from the mundane, busyness from peace. We work ourselves half to death, and anxiety and depression are the norm. Then we try to magically restore ourselves through some ritual behavior, whether it's worship, meditation, reading, exercise, television, or any other habitual balm. Were we to bring together the mundane and the sacred, like the Balinese, we would surely stay more centered in peace.

Many people have tried to do that through Feng Shui, a Chinese and Tibetan science of harmonizing living and working spaces that's extremely popular. It's based on energetic principles similar to those in the Balinese culture. Each of nine sections in the house—and the corresponding sector of every room—represents a certain arena of life. The rear left corner represents wealth and abundance. The rear right represents partnership, both within intimate relationships and in business. The front left represents knowledge and self-cultivation. The front right represents one's supportive allies and the help they give. The center of the space represents the soul and its connection to the earth. The cardinal points of west, north, east, and south represent family, reputation, creativity, and career.

You don't need to be a Feng Shui expert to create a harmonious environment that's a peaceful, appealing haven in a busy world. Yet many businesses and individuals are embracing these principles. Health Communications, the publisher of the wildly successful *Chicken Soup for the Soul* series, arranged their workplace according to the principles of Feng Shui just before the first helping of chicken soup was served. But even if creating harmony in your environment doesn't bring you wealth and success, it will surely bring you peace.

This week, take a good look around at the places where you spend your time. Start with the obvious. Clear out clutter, dead plants, old newspapers, and the like. Rearrange things so that each room feels balanced and peaceful. If the concept appeals to you, read a book on Feng Shui and begin to apply the principles. At the very least, have a go at reorganizing your underwear drawer. Even that is sacred.

16. Create a Refuge

A refuge corner can be a powerful part of your self-care strategy. It's a warm and welcoming place where the demands of life recede and stillness takes over. Like the eye of a hurricane, your refuge space is perpetually calm. When it's filled with meaningful items that bring back memories and associations that are peaceful or sacred, just sitting there is a balm for the soul.

Most people have special pictures, objects, fragrances, candles, or music that support peace, but sometimes we forget about the power of these important resources. A 40-something woman who attended one of the weekend spiritual gatherings that my retreat partner Elizabeth Lawrence and I facilitate, wandered into the Catholic Church attached to the retreat center where we were meeting, late on a Saturday night. Mass was over, but the familiar heady fragrance of incense lingered in the still air.

Although the woman was a religious dropout who hadn't attended Mass in years, the smell brought back associations of peace. She felt comforted, blessed, and lifted beyond the strains of everyday life. The old smells of childhood worship elicited a deep tranquility she had not experienced for years. Although the woman was no longer interested in organized religion, she decided to purchase some of the incense and burn it in a quiet corner of her bedroom that she planned to set aside for inspirational reading, prayer, and meditation. This became her refuge in a busy world.

Any items, sacred or secular, can become power objects for peace. For example, a friend of mine is a fly fisherman. It's his favorite way to relax. The sights and sounds of nature, the flowing water, and the opportunity to focus intently on the habits of the fish fill him with calmness. Fishing, he tells me, is a spiritual experience. His home is filled with fly-fishing memorabilia. To him, the sight of a frame filled with flies he has tied, pictures of favorite fishing spots, and even a reading lamp in a fishing motif transport him back to the comfort of nature. The workbench where he ties his flies is the most peaceful place in his home. He goes there often, just for silent reflection and respite from his busy day.

People often save little talismans associated with peaceful or uplifting experiences. I have a collection of feathers. Some of them were found, while others were gifts. They are especially meaningful because of a night and a day that I spent praying on a sacred mountain. By morning, I had an intense migraine headache. The pain and nausea became almost unbearable as the hot sun of the South Dakota summer beat down relentlessly. I had made an agreement with the Lakota medicine man who was my spiritual guide to stay on the mountain until late afternoon. So even though I was too sick to do much praying, I was determined to at least honor the commitment. At one point, I was huddled miserably on the bed of sage that covered the ground inside the altar in which I was resting. My dehydrated body shook with dry heaves. Suddenly the rush of enormous wings broke the air, and an eagle landed by my side, fanning me and bringing me courage.

Since that day, feathers have become precious objects, and I often find one when I'm feeling stressed. A silver feather necklace has become a portable refuge. Just holding it transports me back to that magic moment on the mountain when I realized that we are never alone. Unseen helpers protect us. A picture of an eagle over my desk brings tranquility and inspiration amidst the intensity of ringing telephones and fax machines, reports to write, and correspondence to answer. A beautiful prayer basket in the corner of the room holds people's requests for help. It is a potent reminder of how important it is to love one another. A small statue of Kwan Yin, the Chinese Bodhisattva of Compassion, silently watches over everything.

A Greek Orthodox friend of mine has a little altar in her living room that holds several precious icons. These spiritual paintings, she says, are like doorways to divine realms. Each one carries its own unique power to uplift, heal, and inspire. Pictures of gods and saints, family and friends, statues and paintings, meditation cushions, prayer shawls, special books and journals, music, and candles or prayer books can all be part of your refuge corner.

This week, think about the things that bring you spiritual comfort. Create a sacred space in your home, even if it's just a small nook. Make sure that every object you place there is intensely meaningful so that the power of the place remains undiluted by clutter. Less is definitely more. Once you've created your refuge, use it only for peaceful activities. Doing your taxes there will imbue it with an entirely different set of associations. If you invest a few minutes a day visiting your refuge, you will experience increased peace all day long. You can take that tranquility with you by carrying one of the sacred objects in your pocket or purse.

17. Nap to Awaken the Genius Within

᯽

"Sleep," wrote Shakespeare, "knits up the raveled sleeve of care." On average, we spend eight hours a day sleeping while the body and mind are repaired and restored. But that sweet restoration can be elusive. One-third of all adult Americans report insomnia each year. Approximately 200,000 car crashes are attributed annually to excessive sleepiness, as well as some notable disasters such as the nuclear meltdown at Three Mile Island.

Most of us have experienced the personal kind of meltdown that poor sleep causes. It lessens appreciation for life, interferes with relationships, and is linked to poor health. Blessed by sound sleep for a lifetime, I developed a heightened sense of compassion for the sleepless during the hormonal storms of menopause that frequently cut my sleep down to three or four restless, sweaty, blanket-tossing hours a night. I wasn't pleasant to be around during that time. Insomnia creates tension and irritability, interferes with concentration, and can lead to depression. In 1995, researchers calculated that the total direct cost of insomnia was $13.9 billion for sleeping medications and doctor visits alone. The indirect costs in terms of decreased ability to function and to problem-solve, as well as absenteeism, make insomnia an economic issue as well as a pressing personal problem.

The reasons for poor sleep are legion. Everything from stress to eating crackers and watching movies in bed—giving the mind the impression that the bed is for play rather than for sleeping—have been investigated. But the studies leave out an obvious culprit. As a society, we are out of rhythm. We were meant to go to sleep when it's dark and to awaken with the dawn. My husband, Kurt, knew an elderly man in West Virginia who lived in a cabin without electricity. Kurt asked him what he did at night, and the man replied, "I go to sleep. That's what we're supposed to do when it gets dark."

But human beings are adaptable creatures. Even with the advent of electric light, most of us have managed to get our rest. But other, more subtle rhythms also get violated in our busy culture. For example, energy tends to cycle down in the afternoon after lunch. Rather than taking a refreshing nap, most of us are more likely to reach for a cup of coffee. Ignoring the body's signals that it's time for rest, we just keep on keeping on. The result is that natural, cyclic patterns of wakefulness and drowsiness get flattened out. As a scientist, my guess, which is properly called a hypothesis, is that disorder in these subtle daytime rhythms contributes to sleep disturbances at night.

As a college student, I had a National Science Foundation fellowship to study cephalopods in scenic Naples, Italy. What that means is that I was a glorified octopus trainer at the Zoological Aquarium. But my eight-armed charges were on their own from noon until four or four-thirty in the afternoon. That was siesta time for the humans. We ate a big lunch and took a nap. Stores were closed and shutters were drawn. It was time to restore our rhythms. Many countries have a tradition of taking siestas. Some American companies are taking a lesson from them and providing nap rooms for employees. Taking a little catnap when your eyes start to close is much more restorative than a shot of espresso.

This week, pay attention to your sleep patterns. Do you feel refreshed in the morning, or are you still tired? Insomnia refers to poor-*quality* sleep as well as to poor *quantity*. If you're fatigued, try the obvious: Get more exercise and cut down on caffeine. Most important, listen to your body. When you're tired, take a nap or try a short meditation, which can be equally restorative. Hang some sort of *Do Not Disturb* sign on your door. *Genius at Work* might do nicely. And it's the truth.

Getting in tune with your body's natural rhythms will make you more creative, productive, and peaceful. Napping awakens the genius within.

18. Just Do It—and Shed Those Bad Habits!

༄ ༀ

Almost everyone has some bad habit they would like to modify. But change is hard. Ask any smoker who's been trying to quit for years. Bad habits drain energy because they make you feel out of control. The flesh may be willing, but the mind is weak. Nevertheless, people do give up bad habits. Alcoholics can recover, dirt-a-holics can learn to pick up their piles, and even perfectionists can take a rest and learn to leave the dirty dishes in the sink overnight. Sometimes breaking a habit can take ten tries or a hundred, but peaceful people are the ones who eventually "bite the bullet" and get over it. Often it just takes a little encouragement to get over the hump. Maybe "Stephanie," a former patient of mine, can inspire you.

Stephanie was a high-powered business consultant at a top firm. Chronic stomach pains had become a way of life, and she joined our stress-disorders program in the hopes that relaxation could do what Pepto-Bismol couldn't. Stephanie assured me that the main source of tension in her life was her autocratic boss. I always take pronouncements like that with a grain of salt. It's easy to blame our troubles on somebody else. There are some people who would complain if Mother Teresa was their supervisor. But as I got to know her, it was obvious that Stephanie wasn't that type of person. If anything, she tended to blame herself when relationships were difficult. She was as smart as a whip and as patient and long-suffering as a stone.

People continually took advantage of Stephanie's easygoing

nature, so she routinely carried more than her share of responsibilities. After several discussions in the group, she realized that her boss was only a symptom of her own problem. And virtually all the people who she worked with were just like her. They had all been hired by the same boss, who had perfect radar for people whom he could take advantage of. The prestige of the firm and the hefty paychecks the consultants received were enough to maintain a sizable, if unhappy, staff.

About six weeks into the ten-week program, Stephanie announced, "I'm biting the bullet. It's time to quit my job. I'm tired of holding the bag for the boss, working myself to the bone, and then getting kicked in the ass. My career as a doormat is done." Cheers went up around the room, and the group initiated a spirited discussion about their own energy-draining physical and emotional habits.

The word *courage* is derived from the French *coeur*, for "heart." Take heart, we say; you can do it. And when you take one small step to improve your life, it's easier to take the next. The nervous system is remarkably flexible. Even the attitudes and habits of a lifetime can be changed. A friend of mine who had been an alcoholic for most of his adult life joined the AA program and got sober. A year later, he used the same 12-step principles to give up a three-pack-a-day cigarette habit. Several months later, at the age of 45, he took up running. Now he participates in marathons.

This week, make a list of the habits that you know get in the way of your inner peace. Bite the bullet and take a step to change one of them, even though you know that it will be uncomfortable. It's easier to make changes if you have an ally, so tell someone you trust implicitly what your intention is. Ask them to check in with you once a week for the next few months. The support will help keep you on track and provide the encouragement you need.

19. Do What You *Can*, Not What You *Won't*

In working with people for many years, I've noticed that one of the prime ways we undermine ourselves is by setting unrealistic goals. Instead of deciding to lose five pounds, you set your sights on losing thirty. Rather than making a commitment to walking for 30 minutes several times a week, you start a 90-minute program of aerobics and weight training. Soon enough, you give up altogether. It's hard to feel peaceful when you think that you're a failure. Self-flagellation sets in. Then, one fine day, you decide to get your life under control once and for all, set another round of unrealistic goals, and repeat the entire mind-bending experience all over again. That's the anatomy of staying stuck.

In the last decade or so, we've been regaled with the importance of diet and exercise. There's more information about these topics than practically anyone wants to know. But has it helped? The sad fact is that Americans are chubbier and more sedentary than ever. One of the reasons for our collective failure to be fit is the familiar tendency to bite off more than we can chew. My very own treadmill spent years as a coat rack for that very reason. Having been a runner in days gone by (before my knees informed the pain centers of my brain that I was ruining their health), a treadmill seemed downright wimpy. If I couldn't run, I reasoned that I could at least walk four 15-minute miles several times a week. Our home, by the way, is near the top of an 8,600-foot mountain in the Colorado Rockies. Just breathing is an aerobic activity up here.

After a few breathless workouts, the treadmill lost its allure. I began to think of it as a torture device. One day, a mere 25 minutes into the grueling routine, the FedEx man came to the door. Saved by the bell! I checked the console of the treadmill, which lists so many vital signs that it could double as an intensive-care unit. About 250 calories had been burned off. Good enough. The next day, I decided to throw caution to the wind and choose a slower walking speed, one that I might actually enjoy. Thirty minutes later, I had burned off almost as many calories, even though the total distance walked was only about a mile and a half. The next day, I realized that I was actually looking forward to the treadmill because a mere 30 minutes at a pleasant clip was fun and easy. I know what you're thinking: No pain, no gain. But the truth is that most of us are not training for the Olympics. We're just hoping to avoid rusting in place.

Whatever your goal may be, try being more than realistic. Set your sights lower rather than higher. By doing so, you increase your chance for success, which motivates you to take the next step when you're ready. Although this is the opposite of the message we're usually given, it's often the best way to get where you're going.

Remember the story of the tortoise and the hare? I once had a yoga teacher who told me to stretch only half as far as I could. His advice helped me relax and let go, enjoying the yoga so that I felt more like doing it.

What are some of the things you want to do but have difficulty sticking with? This week, choose one area that has been elusive, and set a more-than-realistic goal. Do what you honestly *can*, rather than what you probably *won't*. For example, if you eliminated two pats of butter from your diet every day, you would lose about eight pounds in a year. If you walked at a moderate pace for 30 minutes, three times a week, you'd lose another eight pounds. While you might barely notice a weight loss of less than a pound-and-a-half a month, little successes add up to major accomplishments.

20. Focus on Making Small Changes

When you try to change your entire life in a day, chances are slim that you'll succeed, unless you're being taken into the Witness Protection Program. And when you think about the effort that change takes, it can be paralyzing. But there's a much gentler option. Let a story about my friend and colleague Dr. Janet Quinn, author of *I Am a Woman Finding My Voice*, tell you more.

Once upon a time, Janet went to Australia to spend a week with a group of aboriginal elders. One day they piled into a van to search the arid outback for *bush tucker* (Australian for "food"). Items such as Witchety grubs and honey ants may seem unattractive to Westerners, but they're delicacies in the outback.

The van was bouncing along a rutted road when suddenly it slowed way down. There was a camel in front, loping along at its own slow pace. The driver honked. The camel went faster. Then it slowed down again, apparently unconcerned about the van on its tail. The cycle of honking, trotting, and slowing down was repeated over and over again. The sight of Janet imitating the wagging gait of the camel's behind can't be captured in words, but perhaps you get the picture.

As she sat in the van, contemplating the dromedary, it occurred to Janet that there were miles of uninhabited land in every direction, yet the camel stayed on the road. If it had made the tiniest adjustment to its course—even a fraction of a degree—it would have had endless miles of unmolested space to roam in, and there would be respite from the honking and trotting. But apparently the camel hadn't thought this through, and it kept to its uncomfortable course.

A lot of people do the same thing. You may be stressed and unhappy about the course of your life, but you just keep on walking in the same direction. When I've asked people why they don't change their circumstances, the most common response is "fear." They know the box that they're stuck in. Even though it's uncomfortable, it's at least familiar. But if they change, there's a chance that the unknown will be worse than their current situation. The enemy you know seems safer than the enemy you don't know. The second most common reason why people fear change is that they feel overwhelmed by the amount of work it will take. But think of the camel. A change in course of just a fraction of a degree would have resulted in unlimited freedom.

I knew a working mother named "Shawna" whose dream was to become a nurse, but for years she was like the camel and stayed on her old course. She had a lot of valid reasons: School takes time and costs money. How could she and her son possibly survive if she quit work to study?

Then Shawna took a small step. Since her job paid for continuing-education courses at the local community college, she signed up for biology and loved it. The professor alerted her to a scholarship for older women entering nursing, and Shawna applied and was accepted. Student loans covered most of her living expenses, and she waited tables twice a week to cover the rest. Shawna became a nurse during the recent shortage. The hospital she signed on with gave her a cash bonus large enough to pay off most of her loans. One small change . . . and unimaginable opportunities opened up.

Psychologist Ellen Langer discovered that people who try new things are healthier and happier than those who stay in a rut. Even choosing a different route home from work benefits you. In her book, *Mindfulness*, she makes the point that variety keeps us engaged in life. You might be able to zone out if you've taken the same route a hundred times, but if you're on unfamiliar turf, you have to stay tuned in. Tuning in encourages curiosity and results in a more adventurous life. An acquaintance of mine chose to drive a new way to work one day and got rear-ended in a traffic jam. But all's well that ends well. She married the man who slammed into her.

This week, try making two small changes every day. Take a different street to work, turn off the television for an evening, go to a restaurant that serves exotic food, change your brand of toothpaste, smile at someone you don't know, show up at work wearing Groucho Marx glasses, go to a different supermarket, get a more daring hairdo, eat dessert first, or buy or borrow a piece of clothing in a color you never wear. The possibilities are endless.

At the end of the week, reflect on what these little changes produced. Then think about your life. If you're in a rut like Janet's camel, identify one small step you might take toward change. There's a whole lot of landscape to explore once you leave the beaten path.

സ സ സ

PART III

Strategies for
Changing Your
Relationship to Time

21. Understand What Saving Time Really Means

As Americans, most of us are used to running on the treadmill of earn and spend. Time is money; therefore, efficiency is of the essence. In the name of doing more things in less time, the hours and minutes that fill the seasons of our lives can become the enemy. Like sand in an hourglass, we watch it falling away, challenging ourselves to make every grain count. But for what? To scurry around driving ourselves crazy, or to savor the infinite possibilities that lie hidden within time like the germ of an oak tree inside the acorn? Saving time is not a matter of anxiously packing more things into our day, but of experiencing the essence of what unfolds *within* each moment.

Several years ago, I was reading one of the ubiquitous magazine articles about saving time. It was filled with "helpful hints." The author suggested that you conserve precious minutes by soaping your hair only once in the shower instead of twice. Joyous thoughts from my childhood ran through my mind. I remembered sitting in the tub while my mother gently shampooed my hair twice, until it was squeaky clean. I've listened for that squeak, and unconsciously experienced my mother's tenderness, in all the shampoos of my adult life. Nonetheless, I tried the helpful hint and shampooed just once, playing beat-the-clock. I got out of the shower two or three minutes faster all right, but I felt downright testy. Is this what life has come to? A breathless race to an exhausted finish?

The next morning, I decided to resist rushing through my shower. After all, the sensation of warm water and creamy suds is one of life's sweet pleasures. Muscles unwind in the steamy warmth, and you can choose to enjoy the self-massage rather than imitate a three-minute automatic car wash. Not only did I soap my hair twice, but I dawdled, extracting every bit of pleasure possible from this small revolutionary act.

While shampooing mindfully, languorous as a cat, I realized how often I was mindless about what I was doing. I was everywhere but in the moment. Time was running out, and it was doing so without me because I was somewhere else. My body was in one place, going through the motions, but my mind was elsewhere. Even while showering, I was used to being a model of efficiency, planning the day or ruminating about unfinished business while scrubbing away. It was possible to emerge from the shower exuding as much adrenaline as if I'd been fighting off mad Norman from *Psycho*.

Our culture prides itself on this kind of efficient multitasking. We read while we eat, watch television while we study, and think about our problems while driving. No wonder we're so stressed and depressed.

I invite you to try a little experiment, and put your mind fully into one thing.

Let's take the shower as an example. Why not think of it as a meditation rather than a chore, with the moment-to-moment unfolding of delightful sensation and peace your primary focus? Stand under the shower and pay attention to your breathing. Let every out-breath be an opportunity to let go of the past and future so that you can enter more fully into the present. Let the warm water wash over you in delicious waves. Now imagine that it's a waterfall of light, washing fatigue and negativity out through the bottoms of your feet. Wash your hair with loving attention, as you would do for a small child. Whenever you catch your mind wandering, take a deep breath and come back to this simplest of meditations. You'll have more energy and peace all day, even if you didn't win the Indy 500 of showering.

The same principle applies to everything you do. You can carry a stack of dishes to the cupboard with your shoulders hunched up to your ears and a scowl on your face, shaving precious seconds off the race to unload the dishwasher. When you finish, you're likely to feel cranky and used up. No one will appreciate your efficiency. What they *will* notice is that you've turned into a Grinch. Throwing efficiency to the wind, you could take some deep, relaxing breaths and move into the moment, enjoying the feelings in your muscles as you hoist the dinner plates into the cabinet. When you drive, you could slow down and enjoy the scenery, rather than racing to the finish line.

As the saying goes, haste makes waste. Not only are you likelier to drop the dishes or have a car crash if you hurry, but you're wasting the essence of your life. Life is not what happens when your shower's over, when the dishwasher's empty, when breakfast has been eaten, when the kids are in bed, when the report is completed, or when you're off your shift. Life happens *now,* one moment at a time. When you're in that moment, efficiency takes care of itself, time seems to slow down, and life is once again a delight.

This week, pay attention to how you go about the tasks that make up your day. When time efficiency turns to tyranny, make a different choice. Take a few more minutes to taste what you're eating, chewing slowly enough to extract exquisite pleasure out of every morsel. Give a real hug, melting into the person, rather than squeezing the breath out of them with a two-second boa-constrictor clutch. Even if it takes a few seconds or minutes longer to do something mindfully, you'll get more done in the long run if you relax and enjoy each task. You and your life will become one again—and you will come home to yourself.

22. Give Up Perfectionism

୬୮ ୲ଟ

Addicts have a catchy little motto: "Anything worth doing is worth doing to excess." Although socially acceptable, perfectionism is actually an addiction. Like all such traits, one of its functions is to distract you from unpleasant feelings and to keep your mind out of uncomfortable places. There are better ways to do that, like healing the underlying problems so that you can live a fuller, richer life. And since perfection is a human impossibility—because we are infinitely creative— if you insist on perfection, you will unavoidably suffer from poor self-esteem. After all, whatever you did, you could have done it better.

I am a recovering perfectionist, although I do have an occasional slip. It was Christmas morning, and all through the house, everyone was stirring. My two adult sons and I were in a cooking frenzy. An herb loaf was rising in the bread machine. Waffles and sizzling bacon were releasing delicious aromas. Eggs were shirring in their pot. And a fudge cake, so carefully prepared for high altitude in our 8,600-foot Rocky Mountain aerie, was baking in a moderate oven. Instead of making a sheet cake, as the recipe had suggested, we decided to make two 8-inch layers. More festive, we thought.

I had set the oven timer to ring five minutes before the cake was supposed to be done. At the appointed moment, my son Andrei went to the oven, toothpick in hand, to test it. Alas, the cake was practically vaporized. We had forgotten to adjust the time for the change in pans. I felt like a complete failure and was furious at myself for lacking 20-20 baking foresight. I was a Martha Stewart reject, a kitchen clod. We had labored so lovingly over the batter. All the ingredients had been brought to room temperature, and even the melted chocolate had been cooled before adding it to ensure a perfect, moist crumb. The cake was to be one of our contributions to a holiday dinner with friends later that afternoon. And after all the work and planning, we had the equivalent of toasted cardboard.

Everyone in our family knows that, like many high achievers, perfectionism can be a problem for me. And we perfectionists get testy when things don't go our way. Not only do we forsake our own peace of mind, we often ruin everyone else's in the process. Over the years, my husband, Kurt, and the boys have learned to deal with this unpleasant tendency by exaggerating my perfectionism until it seems absurd. That was the way they helped prevent me from becoming the Grinch who stole Christmas.

Andrei began a repetitive chant that we first learned from my brother, Alan: "Terrible thing. Terrible thing. The cake is burned. Terrible thing."

My older son Justin chimed in: "And that's not the only thing. She thinks she didn't make enough bacon. Only 20 pieces for the four of us. Terrible thing. Terrible thing." He looked at his brother. "Why do we bother coming home anyway? What kind of crummy establishment is this?"

My husband, Kurt, joined the chant. "The puppy peed on the floor last night. It was her turn, and she didn't take him out in time. Terrible thing. Terrible thing." By then, we were all holding our sides with laughter. It was just a burned cake, not such a terrible thing at all. Because the exaggeration of my perfectionism was so funny, it was easier for me to let go of my desire that the cake be perfect. We scraped off the burned parts and frosted the remainder with chocolate butter cream frosting. Even cardboard is delicious prepared this way.

When we got to our friends' home, I announced that the cake had been burned and would surely be dry. Oh, well. We agreed that it was beautiful anyway. As for the taste—it would be what it would be. The main thing was that we had enjoyed the process of creating it and that it had been accepted so graciously. The cake was indeed as dry as sawdust, but no one minded. The memory of burning it, and then trying to beautify the scraped carcass, was better than a perfect cake could have ever been. It became part of the family mythology.

There's a profound story by Nathaniel Hawthorne that

has helped me with perfectionism tremendously over the years. It's about a chemist who marries a strikingly beautiful woman with only one slight imperfection. She has a port-wine stain in the shape of a tiny hand on one cheek. He becomes obsessed with finding a cream to fade the birthmark. After many attempts, he finally succeeds. But as the stain fades, so does her life. And as she dies, the grieving husband realizes too late that no perfect thing lasts.

The worst thing about focusing on perfection is that it narrows the mind. Since the chemist's attention was fixed on his wife's birthmark, he could not appreciate her beauty. His obsession robbed him of the ability to love who she was.

Perfectionism is a devilish trait because it pulls you out of the present into the past or the future. Since peace exists only in the present moment, it vanishes when the desire for perfection emerges. "If only I'd taken the cake out of the oven sooner, it would have been perfect. . . . If only I'd packed different clothes, then I could enjoy this trip. . . . When I finally lose ten pounds, then my figure will be just right, and then I'll be happy." In the meantime, you've accepted unhappiness as a fact of life.

This week, recognize perfection for the intruder that it is. If it knocks on your door offering you the devil's bargain—that you will be happy if something turns out just right—try not to take the bait. Label the insidious mind habit: "Here is perfectionism. It's a trap. I can see it and let it go." If you give in to perfectionism anyway and then find yourself unhappy, try exaggerating your predicament with the equivalent of "Terrible thing, terrible thing." Then reflect sanely on your situation. How terrible is it, really? In an hour, a day, a week, or a year, who will care?

Face it—most of the time, no one cares right now.

23. Surrender Your Resistance

Procrastinating about completing a task that you need to attend to is one of the greatest misuses of time. Have you ever dreaded a chore, complaining in anticipation, only to be surprised by how much you actually enjoyed doing it? Cleaning out the refrigerator was a personal case in point for me. It used to be one of those things I put off for as long as possible. But the fridge seemed to take on a life of its own, mocking my unwillingness to clean it every time I opened the door. It's humiliating to lose your peace of mind to an appliance.

One day the orange juice spilled, and rivulets of sticky stuff dripping off the broccoli galvanized me into action. Once I gave in to the dreaded task and began emptying the shelves, it was fun—sort of like a treasure hunt or an archaeological dig. Consolidating the remnants of three jars of apricot jam was almost as rewarding as writing a book—and much more immediate. I was into it, going with the flow, relishing the moment, an invincible warrior. Martha Stewart would have been proud. Closing the sparkling door, it seemed outrageous that I could have wasted so much energy resisting a refrigerator.

Every to-do list is a mix of tasks that are simple and fun (the piece-of-cake category), and things that are real bears. Going out to lunch with a friend is obviously much more inviting than having a root canal or putting the finishing touches on a grant proposal. Getting the enjoyable things done energizes you. Every time you complete a task with even a modicum of goodwill, your mind stops for a moment to congratulate itself, and you feel a little rush of peace and energy. That sets you up to accomplish the next task with some verve, and pretty soon you're firmly anchored in the present moment, enjoying life's to-do lists.

But lurking in the margins of most such lists are a few decidedly unattractive chores. You may try to ignore them, but you know they're there, and they eat up your energy. Because they stay with you until you finish them, these tasks take up considerable mental space and make you feel much busier than you actually are. Even at three in the morning, they're with you. Even while making love, they may be with you. What a paradox that is. The things you dislike the most succeed in taking up the majority of your mental time.

How about making that uncomfortable phone call to apologize to the friend you let down? What about completing the complicated application for new health insurance? Isn't it high time you got the recycling done before the pyramid of bottles in the hall closet topples over and dismembers an innocent bystander? Maybe it would be possible to complete your income tax before the afternoon of April 15. Undone to-do's pull you out of the moment, create stress and tension, and siphon off a lot of juice that could be spent more creatively.

It's been said that whatever you resist, persists. As soon as you dig in and start complaining about how unpleasant a chore is going to be, you automatically feel stress and lose your peace. When you actually get around to the job, more often than not, it's much easier than you thought. Maybe it was even as much fun as cleaning out the refrigerator.

Perhaps there are one or two things that *you're* resisting on your to-do list. Choose one thing that you've been putting off and get it done this week. This may seem like a meager suggestion, but when you build up the habit of surrendering to what you resist, rather than letting undone tasks drain you, life will seem far less busy and much more peaceful.

24. Learn to Say No

Like most women (and some men), saying no makes me feel guilty. There's a nagging sense that if I refuse a reasonable request, I'm being selfish. But we need to distinguish between selfishness and self-care. A no to one thing is a yes to something else. If I decline to read a book manuscript that a stranger hopes I'll endorse, then the time that I set aside for family and friends, for hiking and skiing, and for rest and relaxation is honored. Like most working people, I don't have the luxury of extra time. So I have to be a good steward of the life energy that time represents.

When I was being supervised as a therapist—and receiving my own therapy in the process—learning to say no was a prime issue. My inclination was to give time and attention to practically anyone who asked. The only one I could comfortably said no to was myself. So the supervising therapist used an entire 50-minute session helping me learn how to say yes to myself by saying no to others.. He would make various requests, and whatever they were, I had to refuse.

"Would you please come over to my house and clean the bathrooms?" It was easy enough to say no to that. But when he got to things like, "I'm short of cash this week and my children are hungry. Can I borrow a hundred dollars?," I was stymied. Every fiber in my being wanted to give him the money, even though it was only an exercise. I began to justify myself and make excuses as to why it was impossible to honor his request. His response was short and incisive.

"Stop that right now! You don't have to justify yourself. You're entitled to your own opinions and decisions because you're a human being worthy of respect. Stop explaining yourself, and stand in that place inside where you know that you're worthwhile. You say yes so that people will love you, and that's the problem. Hear me. *You* are enough. You don't have to keep buying people's love. And if you won't stop, you will be useless as a therapist, a friend, a lover, or a parent—because you'll never be able to tell the truth or set appropriate boundaries for other people's behavior. You are a doormat."

That was clear. We agreed that I would carry out an assignment in saying no the following week. I actually signed a contract vowing that it would be completed as agreed. Let me give you the background. As a cancer researcher and expert in the mind/body connection, I had begun to receive a fair number of unsolicited book manuscripts. People often requested that I read their book-to-be and provide an endorsement for the back cover. I take these requests seriously, and saying yes can mean 10 or 12 hours of work. Added to the rest of my busy life, these manuscripts became a nightmare. Just the sight of one could strike terror in my heart. Nonetheless, I often read them because so many were worthwhile. I wanted to help.

The week of the assignment, I gave a lecture at a medical conference. As I was stepping down from the stage, a woman approached me, manuscript in hand. She was an unexpected survivor of advanced ovarian cancer. Having beaten the odds, she was overflowing with gratitude and told me tearfully that I had been an important part of her recovery. Now she was thrilled to close the circle and have me read her story. I was mortified. The contract flashed in front of my eyes. With a pounding heart and a dry mouth, I summoned up the courage and as kindly and gently as possible, declined to read her manuscript without justifying myself.

The poor woman went berserk. She accused me of being a fraud who didn't care about anyone but myself. Then she stomped off, leaving a group of wide-eyed bystanders in her wake. While I'm prone to say that God has an uncanny sense of humor, this particular joke was over the top. The timing was impeccable. In retrospect, the intense discomfort was worthwhile because it made me face the worst possible scenario. She had been in a rage, and still I survived. That encounter was a turning point. Although it's still sometimes hard to say no, I *can* do it when it's the most skillful choice.

"No" is a boundary that's like an emotional immune system. Your physical immune system has one primary function that biologists refer to as distinguishing "self" from "not-self." Its job is to keep out invaders such as bacteria, viruses, and parasites. The immune system maintains the integrity of the body so that it can work optimally. But sometimes it makes an error and mistakes self for not-self. This results in an autoimmune condition such as arthritis or multiple sclerosis in which the body destroys part of itself. That's just what we do to ourselves emotionally when we can't say no.

This week, pay attention to the way you respond to requests. Some people say no too hastily. Others say yes too readily. If you feel that you're out of balance in either direction, take your time before answering whenever you can. "Let me think about it" is an option that can give you the time to reflect and make an authentic decision about the best course of action. In the long run, this strategy will give you peace and power, even if in the short run your response is not what the other person wants to hear.

25. Live in Rhythm Time

☜☞

Western culture thinks of time as linear. Its passage is a little bit like walking the plank on a pirate ship. We are born, we walk the plank of time, and then we die and fall off the end. Days are linear as well. We start our day at a certain hour in the morning and finish it at a later hour that night. Tasks are strung out along the time line in their specified order.

But other cultures approach time in a much gentler, more rhythmic way. Time and tasks move together in a subtler kind of relationship. My husband, Kurt, and I visited such a culture one winter. We were sitting in a round outdoor pavilion perched on a cliff, overlooking the tranquil waters of Maho Bay, on the Caribbean Island of St. John. Pelicans were dropping gracefully from the air, diving for fish. A chorus of melodic birdsong rose on the wings of the morning. But I was not yet fully present to the abundance of nature's mercy. Part of me was still catching up, having traveled across three very linear time zones.

Holistic physician Stephan Rechtschaffen, author of *Timeshifting*, introduced the workshop/vacation week where I was on the faculty. He delved into the topic of "island time" and how it takes a little while to shift from our busy lives into a slower rhythm.

He told a story about a ferry that used to deliver produce to the islands. A sign on its side read, "We leave sharp, Thursday." That's island time. Things happen at the appropriate moment, when all forces come together in harmony, rather than at an arbitrary, appointed moment.

American Indian culture has a similar relationship to time. I once gave a talk for the Navajo Health Service in Winslow, Arizona. My lecture was scheduled to begin at 9 A.M. I was ready, chomping at the bit, busy and precise professional that I am. But the specified hour came and went. People kept filtering in. They visited in little groups with great delight. Then, somewhere around mid-morning, the room was slowly and lovingly smudged with sage. I was getting antsy. They had paid me to speak, and I was determined to give them their money's worth—hopefully soon.

At about 10:30, the conference officially got under way, but not with my keynote address. The group gathered in a circle for a greeting dance. By the time it was over, I had almost given up on the idea of lecturing altogether. But just before lunch, the time was finally right. We were entrained in a collective rhythm—of one mind. I gave my talk to a receptive, harmonious group. They were in a state totally different from the uptight participants at most other conferences, where starting the program a couple of minutes late—let alone a few hours late—might have fueled an insurrection.

Some of us worry, plan, and compete in increments of time even smaller than hours or minutes. We have nanoseconds to contend with. But when clock time obscures rhythm, the result we want is easily lost.

Stephan Rechtschaffen told a story about a woman who wanted to make sure that she saw as many tropical fish as possible while snorkeling in St. John. She bought a plastic-laminated fish chart and a waterproof marker. She could then check off each fish she observed. Unfortunately, there were none to be seen. So she swam faster. The fish seemed to be in hiding. So she swam faster still. Finally exhausted, the woman just gave up and floated. The moment that she surrendered her aggressive idea of time to the rhythm of the sea, the fish came out of hiding.

I wonder how much time we waste and how much busyness we create by thrashing around like predators, rather than surrendering to the flow. Over the years, I've adopted the strategy of living on rhythm time whenever possible. Instead of approaching my to-do list in a linear way, I let it approach me. If the rhythm of life favors cleaning the closets rather than returning phone calls, that's what gets done. If I feel like writing, rather than doing the books, I surrender to that urge. Cooperating with the confluence of forces that arises in the moment is one of the essential secrets of efficiency and peace.

Modern life is such that sometimes we have to do things that are not in the rhythm. Perhaps the quarterly taxes are due and you just received the final documentation, maybe the children need a ride, or perhaps a certain phone call has to be made right away. Some things realistically can't wait. But many things can. You may have a month to write an article, or a window of two weeks to file insurance forms. If you wait for the right rhythm, rather than assigning tasks an arbitrary linear time slot, life can be easier and much more pleasant.

The essence of right relationship to time is flexibility, which is also a powerful measure of mental health. Can you change your plans when the forces of life come together in a pattern that's different from the one you intended?

This week, try taking a rhythm-time approach to your to-do list. I'm not advocating procrastination or chaos. Instead, I'm inviting you to approach life like a melody, rather than one note at a time. Your tasks will still get done—but the result will be more creative and elegant. And you will surely be more peaceful.

26. Take Time for Simple Pleasures

"I had the time of my life" is a way of saying that you really enjoyed yourself. But if joy is a valid measure of time, the average lifetime is pretty short. So much of our days are filled with working and spending—and then getting up and doing it all over again—that the simple pleasures that give life meaning are too often ignored.

For example, gardening is one of my favorite activities, but well-meaning friends once tried to talk me out of it in a misguided way of trying to get me to simplify. About 20 years ago, our family went on a week-long trip, and the friends volunteered to house-sit. When we returned from our vacation, we were subjected to an uninvited lecture about the value of simplicity (which stemmed from a lecture their minister had given the previous Sunday).

It seems that my huge collection of houseplants was the target of our friends' call to simplify. Caring for all the greenery had been a big chore for them. "Give your plants away," they counseled, "and you'll have more time and peace." But for what?

Their unsolicited advice fell short of the mark. While dealing with the plants was obviously a drain on them, it was an energizer for me. I loved turning them so that all the leaves were kissed by light, watching their new growth emerge, knowing how much to water each one, and tucking them into new pots when the old ones were outgrown. I carried a plastic bag and a Swiss army knife in my purse in case the opportunity arose to take a cutting from some interesting specimen. Even picking off the occasional mealy bug was fulfilling. In short, I was a plant maniac and still am. Nurturing plants is a way of nourishing my soul. Giving them away in the service of simplicity would have been foolish. They are, in themselves, one of the simple pleasures that can bring joy and peace to life.

Simplicity is less about the number of material things you own than it is about maintaining the pleasures that knit you into the sturdy fabric of life. While television can be a pleasure when it energizes, encourages, instructs and inspires, too often it is a passive way to zone out. After a night of watching television, you rarely hear, "Wow, that was so great. I had the time of my life." True pleasures reconnect you to the web of life, rather than disconnecting you and dropping you into an electronic twilight zone.

Like most busy people, I have to use time consciously or work will expand to fill almost every waking hour. And I have to use money consciously or paying for unnecessary possessions will exhaust me. But each one of us makes choices. Filling the bird feeder requires money and effort, but there's nothing like the sight of a downy woodpecker, or a couple of blue jays squabbling, to lift my spirits. And I still love to care for plants, indoors and out. Watering and dead-heading boxes of petunias throughout the summer is demanding, but the work involved is far outweighed by the abundance of purple, red, and pink blooms. In the spirit of simplicity, our menagerie would definitely have to go. But the four dogs, walking hairballs that they are, are a source of constant fun and companionship.

This week, think about the simple pleasures that give you the time of your life. Walk around your house and take stock. Do your possessions energize you, or are they a drain? If you own things that are more trouble than they're worth, simplification is in order. That's why God invented garage sales. If you're a habitual television watcher and want to discover more simple pleasures this week, try a TV fast. Lots of time will open up. Spend it with your loved ones making music, reading, painting, repotting your plants, baking a batch of cookies, tending a fish tank, or any hobby that needs time and care. Life is lived in the small places, the in-between spots whose magic lies in their capacity to reconnect us to our souls.

27. Choose Wisely: Time or Things

༄ ༅

I have an acquaintance who lives by the adage, "When life gets tough, the tough go shopping." The busier and more stressed she is, the more time and money she spends trying to distract herself in the malls and boutiques of greater Boston. The result is that both she and her husband have to work harder to support her spending sprees. Her husband is in his 60s and would like to retire, but he keeps on working to pay her bills. The stress this has caused in their marriage has nearly brought it to the breaking point.

The average American has a similar problem, carrying almost the equivalent of their annual income in credit card debt. Sure, getting something you want feels wonderful for a brief time, but the problem is that the happiness is transient. Before you can say, "Wow, I'm so excited about my new computer!," you're off in search of a new VCR. How easy it is to become a slave to desires, mistaking an external object for the internal state of peace that is every heart's true desire.

There's an old story about a drunk crawling around on his hands and knees, earnestly searching for his keys underneath a street lamp. When a Good Samaritan stops to help, he wants to know where, exactly, the keys were lost. The drunk weaves around a bit, and then points excitedly to a spot several hundred feet down the road.

"Then why are you looking for them here?" the passerby asks incredulously.

"Because the light's better," replies the drunk.

So it is with looking for peace through buying and spending, mistaking an internal state for an external possession.

My mother, may her pessimistic but realistic soul rest in peace, had the right idea about shopping. She loved it and hunted down bargains with the best of them, but she didn't expect material things to make her happy or peaceful. A game of Scrabble with her family was a better choice. She was honest about shopping and used to say that it's simply easier to be miserable in nice surroundings. She had accepted the idea that most people drive themselves crazy with want and worry, so why not do it in style, since she could at least afford what she bought. Like many people in her generation, if she couldn't pay for something in cash, she didn't buy it. With the exception of homes and cars, which few of us can pay for with cash, that's still the best policy.

There are things you need and things you want. There are also things that you want, but will probably rarely use once you get them. Like a glut of Christmas toys, they will gather dust in a closet.

This week, if visions of new possessions start to dance in your mind, ask yourself, "Why do I really want this?" If the answer is because you honestly require it, have a great time satisfying the need. If you want it, can afford it, and it will bring you lasting pleasure, it may be a reasonable choice. But if the answer is that you're trying to chase away boredom, loneliness, busyness, or emptiness through buying and spending, be realistic. The happiness will fade, but the credit card bills will flourish. And they can really do a number on your time and peace of mind.

28. Take Time to Get Organized

A simple cause of wasted time and money is lack of organization. I have one friend who, when she cleaned out her closet, realized that she had ten pairs of black slacks. Two or three would have done nicely, but her clothes were so crowded that she'd lost track of what she had. But clutter extracts a more important, energetic toll. When the space you occupy is filled with old, forgotten, or useless items, it's like living in a polluted swamp. The deadwood blocks fresh energy from entering; stagnation sets in.

One summer, I needed a new outfit to make a presentation in Florida. My friend "Ruth," a busy family court judge, decided to change hats and act as a personal shopper. She sat me down in a chair, brought me a glass of water, and flitted efficiently through the store, picking up a variety of clothes that she thought might suit me. I'm a hit-and-run shopper who barely spends more than a few minutes doing what I consider a noxious task, so this was a new experience.

Ruth questioned me: "What's missing in your wardrobe? Let's pick up things that will complement what you have so that you can mix and match them with each other. It will be much easier for you to pack for business trips that way. You're busy enough without worrying about what to wear."

She was right, but who knew what I had? My closet was in a jumble. I admitted that no matter what I bought, there never seemed to be anything to wear. Something was always a little bit off. Ruth stroked her chin and nodded sagely. The clothes judge was about to render a serious verdict. She sadly opined that my wardrobe was guilty and past redemption. When the shock had passed, we picked out some basic pieces of clothing that could be combined in numerous ways. My plan was to rush home and cram them into the closet with all of their dead and dying relatives. If I leaned hard enough on the door, they just might fit.

"Now," Ruth announced, "we need to go up the mountain and sort through all your clothes." Busy as she was, this was a stunningly thoughtful gift of time and attention. It brought tears to my eyes. But soon enough, the tears of gratitude would be replaced by tears of exhaustion. The woman meant business.

Ruth was a ruthless and efficient organizer. We emptied everything out of my closet and then cleaned and refreshed it by burning sage, an herb used by many American Indian tribes to clear out old energy. Then she made me try on every last thing I owned—and in seemingly infinite combinations. There is no point having something in your closet, she instructed me, unless you know what to wear *with* it and how to accessorize it—otherwise, you've wasted your time and money. I winced, thinking about how much had really been wasted on clothing that was mindlessly chosen, didn't suit me, and which had barely been worn. Out of guilt, I tried to keep these items, but Ruth snatched them away, piercing me with what I've come to think of as "The Look."

The giveaway pile grew to the size of a small hill. It was a good thing we'd gone shopping! Then she started in on the belts and scarves, umbrellas and tote bags, shoes, and even socks. No piece of underwear was safe in her presence. She had transformed into a fearsome, devouring goddess of cleanliness and organization. Every nook and cranny, drawer and box in the room was emptied, cleaned, and saged. Then she started in on the bathroom. By that time, I was hardly standing. Not even the jars of nail polish escaped her scrutiny. Finally, every last tube of toothpaste and box of dental floss had found its proper home.

Ruth was true to her word. Now when I pack my suitcases four or five times a month, I know exactly what to bring. Dressing is far simpler, and I look much better. Since very little is left in the closet or in the drawers, it's easy to pick out clothing and create outfits by mixing and matching, rather than doing more shopping. But, at a deeper level, the cleaning ritual was part of moving out the stagnant energy of my life, creating space for something new to come in.

Ruth knew that in the previous year I'd felt my creativity dwindling and had lost some of my focus and vision. She suggested that I sit inside my clean and empty closet and think about what my purpose in life was. Creating an empty space, and then affirming the newness that would flow in, was like a prayer. I know that her tactics might seem offbeat, but they yielded almost immediate results. Only a few days after the cleaning, the opportunity to do a Public Television pledge special, and get my message to a larger audience, suddenly materialized. Letting go of the old had truly made room for the new.

The closet- and drawer-cleaning ritual primed the pump for an even bigger anti-clutter and renewal campaign. I systematically tackled every room in the house—remodeling a few in the process—over the next several months. The big dig is now in its final phase. The house is well organized, spare, and a pleasure to be in. The extraneous knicknacks have either moved on to other people's homes or are decomposing in a landfill. The reorganization has been an exciting and energizing project. And who knows what amazing opportunities will come in its wake?

A former psychology professor of mine once observed that the state of your drawers is a clear reflection of the state of your unconscious. I believe he was correct. As I cleaned and organized my home, unfinished psychological business came up. I had the opportunity to take a closer look at some of my relationships, and to make them better. The space outside of you is a reflection of your inner space. So, if you want more inner peace, take the time to establish outer peace.

This week, start clearing out stagnant energy by checking through your closets and drawers. Lay out your clothing so that you can see everything, and then try it all on. That's the only way to get on intimate terms with what's been hiding in there. If you haven't worn something in a year (other than garments such as wedding and funeral attire that are kept for special occasions), give it to a friend or donate it to an agency. While you're clearing and sorting, think about the fact that you're moving the stagnant energy out of your life. Let your cleaning be an affirmation of new ideas and possibilities. It could be the start of something big.

෴ ෴ ෴

PART IV

Strategies for
Managing Your Mind

29. Make the Mind Your Ally Instead of Your Enemy

You can change your habits and learn to manage your time, but without learning to manage your mind, inner peace is impossible. Even when you're sitting in a comfortable living room, surrounded by loved ones and trying to relax, your mind is capable of producing outrageously stressful mental movies. You probably create them several times a day, perhaps without even noticing what you're doing. The key to making your mind your ally, rather than your enemy, is to become aware of how you produce and direct your very own cinema of the absurd. Then you can choose to run a different feature. Awareness and choice are the keys to mental peace.

Here is how the average stressful mental movie gets produced. I was on my way to facilitate a weekend workshop at a cozy conference center in upstate New York. It had just snowed, and the trees were bowed to the earth, shaking off their frosty offerings in a light breeze. The sunlight sparkled off the flakes, and the world was enchanting in its beauty. I was in the moment, feeling spacious and present. My body was relaxed and comfortable. Then I had some constricting, afflicting kinds of thoughts: *What perfect skiing weather. I moved to Colorado to spend more time outdoors. Everyone at home is probably out enjoying the snow. I'm on my way to spend the weekend teaching indoors. Poor, poor pitiful me. I'm so busy.*

One moment I had been peaceful, expansive and present, thoroughly enjoying life; the next moment I was feeling deprived, crabby, and stressed. Nothing had changed except my thoughts, but that's where we live the majority of our lives. Much of the time, the suffering and busyness we feel has very little to do with the reality of the situation. It's a direct result of our thinking.

The Buddha had a great analogy. He said that each of us has some suffering, like a cup of salt. If you choose to dissolve your salt in a small bowl, the water will be undrinkable. But if you dissolve it in a lake, the water will still taste sweet. The mind—and how you deal with your thoughts—is the equivalent of the bowl or the lake.

Life is filled with very real suffering. God forbid that you or a loved one gets seriously ill, a child dies, your business fails, divorce rips your family apart, or you're betrayed by a person you trust. These things happen because they're a part of life. As you get older, you realize that there's no magic amulet or formula that prevents suffering. Bad things routinely happen to good people. Suffering is part of the human condition. You may wish that this were not so. There are plenty of books that trade on that hope, dispensing advice on how to think, eat, pray, and behave in order to avoid suffering, but suffering will come just the same, in spite of your best efforts. The only thing you can really control is how you respond to life's inherent challenges.

However, there are two types of suffering—mandatory and optional. On my drive through the snowy countryside, there was no external cause for suffering. It was all in my mind. This made me recall that the original definition of yoga had nothing to do with stretching exercises. It was defined as learning how to control the mind and banish the afflicting thoughts that create needless suffering. Learning how to do that, said the ancient sages, is the most difficult of all disciplines. Learning to walk on water was said to be much easier.

Getting control of your thinking may not be easy, but if you want lasting peace, it's a worthwhile practice. As Pogo once said, "We have met the enemy and he is us." It takes consistent effort to overcome that internal enemy, but you can do it as part of your daily life. It takes no more time to use your thoughts well than it does to let them drive you crazy. The basic skills of awareness and choice are available to every person, in every situation, during every hour of the day and night.

For example, in order to stop my mind from creating suffering over its preference to go skiing, I had to notice what I was doing. That is awareness. "Uh-oh. I've lost it. I've made myself miserable." The thought of skiing started the process of woolgathering, or bringing up other thoughts about how busy I was. The next move in the practice of mental martial arts was to change my thinking.

Modern cognitive psychologists suggest that you internally yell, "Stop it," then start in on a more productive train of thought. In the skiing example, I might have nudged my mind onto a better road by thinking, *Next weekend I'll definitely go skiing with my family. I'm glad I remembered how much we love to do that. Today I'm going to enjoy my work.* These thought corrections are called *affirmations.* I like to think of them as station breaks for the opposing point of view. This might all seem very simple, but it's not easy. If it were, we would all be yogis.

This week, notice your thinking and develop the habit of awareness. Witness your thoughts with the recognition that you are *not* your thoughts. They are just a mental movie, and you can make the choice to run another film. Try saying an emphatic mental "Stop it" when you feel tense and constricted by unproductive obsessing. Then substitute a train of thought that can be your ally in experiencing inner peace.

30. Exaggerate the Negative

꿔껗

Remember the song "Accentuate the Positive, Eliminate the Negative"? Easy for them to say! Although being aware of your thoughts, and exercising your authority to choose new ones is helpful, sometimes the strategy of accentuating the neg-ative creates such a hilarious parody of the situation that it can help you change your mind even faster.

Woody Allen films are funny because he understands the movies of the mind. Listening in on the soliloquies of his characters and witnessing their mental concoctions is amus-ing because it's so human. We all do it. One of his characters may have a simple headache and suddenly he fantasizes about being in the hospital with a terminal brain tumor. Psycholo-gist Albert Ellis calls this *awfulizing*. That's a great word. It's powerful because it's such a perfect description of obsessive worrying. Whenever we work up a situation mentally to the point where it has the most dire conclusion imaginable, we're awfulizing.

When I got the contract for this book, I only had two months to write it between business trips. How could I do it? I was already busy, and the daily office work would still be there. Furthermore, the Thanksgiving, Christmas, and New Year's holidays were coming up. Most of our blended family, consisting of six adult children, was planning to visit. I began to awfulize. How could I possibly find time to write? I would miss being with the kids, and they would think they didn't matter. I began to dwell on the fantasy that I was a hypocrite, one of those people who loves everyone in general, but no one in particular. How could I write about inner peace for busy peo-ple if *I* was a mess?

I sat down at the computer to write in that elevated state of mind. Wonder of wonders, after a whole day, nothing but drivel had appeared. That scared me even more. Apparently my fantasies about not being able to write the book were true. So I decided to try exaggerating the negative. "I will never write this book. I'll have to give back the advance and then the bank will repossess the house. We'll end up in the street—and all because those kids are coming!" I can do a pretty good comedy routine, and soon I was laughing so hard that I relaxed. At that point, I was able to acknowledge what my good friend Janet told me. She pointed out that I've always written best under pressure, being the type of person who lives for deadlines.

"If you had a whole year to write this book," she reminded me, "you'd start the month before it was due." I was awfulizing over nothing. I did love to work like that. I could spend the mornings writing and have the rest of the day free once the kids arrived. I relaxed, sat down, and immediately began to enjoy the creative process.

The key to exaggerating the negative is that humor counteracts the physical effects of the stress and panic that accompany obsessive worry. The body can't tell the difference between what you imagine and what is real. Awfulizing is just like watching a scary movie. Your heart pounds, your breathing becomes shallow and ragged, your muscles tense, and you become hyper-alert. You're ready to fight for your life. Once you're in that state, it can be hard to get hold of yourself without a good dose of laughter to calm you down.

You don't have to be facing a book deadline or any other unusual circumstance to get trapped by awfulizing. You probably do it every day. Perhaps you're drinking your morning coffee when you think, *I'm so incredibly busy. I still have yesterday's phone calls to return. I bet there will be 10 new voice-mails and 20 new e-mails today. Then there are the two reports that are due. What a beautiful day it is. I'd love to go out for a walk, but there's too much to do. How did things get so out of control? I'd rather pack it all in and move to a cabin in the woods.* Now that your thinking has created stress, physical tension, and neurotransmitter disaster, you still have to get through your to-do's, but with a body that has just been beaten up by chemical two-by-fours.

This week, when you notice obsessive worry, label it: "I'm awfulizing!" Try exaggerating your movie as if you were Woody

Allen, until you see how entertaining you are. "I'm so busy. No one in the entire history of this world has ever been so busy. I have more phone calls to return than the president. I could run three countries, and I haven't even had breakfast yet." This will help stop the stress response and return you to a relative state of peace.

31. Mind Your *P*'s and *C*'s to Be an Optimist

Some people awfulize more than others do. Those of us who fantasize about happy outcomes are most likely optimists. When our tendency is to think the worst, we're probably pessimists. My mother was the latter. She complained about everything and saw the world as a threat. An infinite number of disasters was just waiting to occur. My brother, Alan, ten years my senior, can remember going to school with a camphor bag around his neck to ward off germs. It apparently warded off friends as well. Our little family lived in the Land of Lysol, east of the Land of Famine, which is where my mother expected we would wind up when another Depression hit.

Given my family history, it may not be surprising that I've had to fight off pessimism all my life. It never really goes away, just as a reformed alcoholic's desire to drink merely waits in the wings. Every day, in every way, I have to maintain my recovering pessimist's attitude. This means that I have to beware of what psychologist Martin Seligman, the author of *Learned Optimism*, calls the three *P*'s. These are not the three little pigs. They refer to the way that pessimists explain why bad things happen.

Let me give you an example. When my three children were young, I took them out for a ride in a new motorboat. We lived near a tidal river in Massachusetts, but knew nothing about boating. The big red-and-green barrels that bobbed in the fast current were a mystery. Oh, well. After a day's frolic in the Atlantic, we headed back up-river toward our dock and promptly ran aground. That was the moment when we realized that the barrels marked the navigable channel and kept you out of reach of sandbars and sea serpents.

It was getting cold and dark. If you were the mother in charge of this outing, what would you think? I not only began to awfulize, but also to blame myself for the catastrophe. It would be 12 more hours and the middle of the night before the tide was high again and we could float free. We might freeze. I imagined the children dying from hypothermia all because I was a careless mother. How could I have gone boating when I didn't know about barrels? Only a bad mother would do that. And I'd missed the last two PTA meetings on top of it! Working mothers might as well be shot. If the children even survived, they were probably ruined anyway. It was all my fault. What a worthless worm I was.

Meanwhile, my son Justin was fairly crowing with delight. I looked up in amazement, hoping to see the Harbor Master with a towboat. What I saw was a pumped-up 14-year-old, so excited about the adventure of saving his family that it was the high point of his young life. He was in the flow, centered in the part of himself that was in harmonious relationship to boats, tides, lines, and seafaring lore. Justin ordered us out of the boat, cast the anchor, and simply hauled us into deeper water. We survived wet thighs with no permanent damage.

My thinking about why we ran aground was a clear example of the three P's. First, I took the incident *personally* and blamed myself. Second, my bad mothering was not limited to this one circumstance. I saw it as *pervasive*. I messed up in many different ways. Third, my incompetence was *permanent*, the story of my life.

Justin explained the situation to himself in a totally different way. His story was about mastery. Whereas I saw the situation as a threat, he saw it as a *challenge.* I felt helpless; he felt empowered and in *control.* While I beat myself up for not knowing about the barrels, he had a *commitment* to a much bigger picture. We might have done better to know about the barrels, but Justin's worldview is that mistakes are the mother of wisdom. His commitment, or guiding principle, is that life is about learning.

Justin's attitude about the boating incident can be summarized by the three *C's*: challenge, control, and commitment. According to psychologist Suzanne Ouellette, those are the attitudes of hardy, optimistic people.

As a recovering pessimist, I have to catch the tendency to *P* on myself, and try to *C* things differently. (Sorry, but it will help you remember the lesson.) One of the ways I do this is to call upon an inner mentor. I know several hardy souls: Justin; my brother, Alan; and my friend Janet are prime examples. When faced with a difficult situation in which I regress into pessimism, I think, *What would Justin or Janet or Alan do about this?* It really helps. You realize that your thoughts are just thoughts; they are not reality. You can change your mind and turn a difficult situation into an exciting, empowering challenge.

What is your own attitude when things don't go your way? Are you an optimist or a pessimist? Read this entry to a friend, and compare notes. This week, be a careful observer of how you explain why bad things happen—even the smallest things. Did you mobilize the three *P's*, or the three *C's*? If you lean toward pessimism, try adopting an inner mentor who can be a powerful ally for maintaining peace and control in a busy world. If your friend is willing, make a plan to report to each other on your progress. It's much easier to make changes if you have the support of someone who cares.

32. Reframe That Problem

૪ ૨

Even when a situation can't be changed, your mental frame of reference *can*. Is your busy day a nightmare, or is it evidence that your business is thriving? Is your assertive two-year-old a monster-in-the-making, or does she just have a mind of her own? Seeing things from a different and more flexible perspective is a great tool to have in your mental bag of tricks.

I once visited a wonderful church in southern California. The minister was so wise and charismatic that several thousand people showed up every Sunday morning. There were three services to accommodate the crowd. They ran short of chairs at the last seating, and the ushers were trying to settle people into the few remaining places. Several minutes after the service was supposed to begin, the shuffling continued. The congregation began to get restless. One of the ushers finally stepped up to the microphone and announced, "Isn't it wonderful that so many people turned out this morning? If you're disturbed about starting a few minutes late, we cordially invite you to change your mind." The crowd laughed and relaxed. They began to acknowledge how marvelous it was that so many people had come.

Every day presents choices about the frame of reference through which you choose to see things. Is a traffic jam so annoying that you need to lean on the horn and swear, or can it be a time to relax, breathe, and listen to a CD? Is the dirt in the front hall a reason to whine, or is it just part of having a dog with large, muddy paws that you love dearly?

In addition to the many small frames of reference, there are big ones that accompany you through life. One person chooses to be upset until the day she dies because her working mother rarely made dinner for the family. Another attributes her love of cooking to the exact same circumstances.

Most individuals have a few chronic problems that reframing can alter. Let's take weight as an example. You probably know people who have been dieting for most of their adult lives and just keep piling on the pounds. That's what makes fad diets so popular. Deep in our hungry little hearts, we all know that the only way to lose weight and keep it off is to eat fewer calories and get more exercise. But if sane eating makes you feel chronically deprived, you're likely to binge. So the diet cycle will continue unless you can think about eating in an entirely different way.

Reframing a problem can radically change both thinking and behavior. The thought, "I better not eat those potato chips—they'll go directly to my thighs," frames food as trouble. One of life's little pleasures becomes a pain. So, instead of thinking about what you *shouldn't* eat to avoid getting fat, you can shift the frame of reference to all the good things that you *get* to eat in order to stay thin.

I make a game out of eating three servings each of fruit and vegetables every day. I think of these as the Six Freggies. As long as I eat all six, I can have anything else I want. In order to eat all those good things, I have to make conscious choices. Cereal with a large bowl of mixed, fresh berries counts for two Freggies, while bacon and eggs are a zero. A mid-morning banana or apple brings the count to three. A salad, soup, or a stir-fry with plenty of vegetables for lunch might bring the count to five. A handful of baby carrots in the afternoon brings me to six. Then I can eat pizza for dinner with a clear conscience. If you reframe eating in a similar way, you can lose weight while making healthier choices.

This week, think of at least one problem that causes you chronic stress. Consider how you might reframe it. Perhaps it's a blessing that you haven't heard from your adult children for a few weeks. If they were in jail, they probably would have called. And just think of the benefits of driving an old clunker. You save a lot on insurance compared to a new car, and there are no worries about fender-benders. They just add to its charm.

33. Ask Yourself, "Am I Having Fun Yet?"

One of my best friends is the brilliant humorist, social commentator, and Erma Bombeck of stress, Loretta LaRoche. Her Public Television specials, books, and lectures have helped millions of people lighten up and see themselves in an amusing way. I call Loretta "Her Holiness, The Jolly Lama." As she says, "Life is a joke, and you are it."

In her irreverent book on the absurdities of modern existence, *Life Is Not a Stress Rehearsal*, Loretta inserts a series of hypothetical tombstones. She suggests that you think about yourself on a typical busy day. What might your tombstone say? "Got everything done, dead anyway"?

When we were kids, having fun and being in the moment was easy. We smiled and laughed a lot. Silliness was in. We were creative and thought outside the box because we refused to get *into* the box. But as adults, we have Responsibilities. We begin to get warped and think things such as, "When I finish all my chores, then maybe I can have some fun." But by the time we're done, it's either time to go to bed, we're too tired, or we're dead.

It's strange to say, but society rewards the glum and humorless. The busier and more miserable we are, the more important we must be. I once had a patient who came to our mind/body clinic because she had chronic urinary tract infections. The reason was simple. She had a position as the manager of an up-and-coming biotech firm. She told me, with great pride, that she purposely refrained from drinking fluids at work to stay dehydrated. Then she wouldn't have to waste time peeing. This was supposed to give her staff the idea that she was responsible, serious, and business minded. They should be the same way.

Fortunately, synchronicity struck. The day before the dehydrated manager came to see me, some joker had photocopied a very official-looking announcement and put one in the mailbox of each member of my own department. The memo was entitled: "Departmental Rules for Going to the Bathroom." The document included detailed instructions for getting permission from your supervisor, limiting your visits to the rest room to only twice per day, and only using the sanctioned number of toilet paper squares. Although the memo was hilarious, several stressed co-workers actually took it seriously. My patient, fortunately, saw the humor when I showed her the memo. We had a good laugh together, and she left the days of chronic urinary tract infections willingly behind her.

In the interest of controlling themselves and others, a lot of busy people restrain not only their bladders, but their spontaneity and joyfulness, too. They can't remember how to have fun. I once teamed up with two performing-artist friends to facilitate a five-day women's workshop. Our idea was to run a mini summer camp where women could laugh, sing, dance, and be creative, leaving their busy lives temporarily behind. Having broken out of the "life-is-so-serious" box, we hoped that they would go home with permission to lighten up. As the week went on, it was delightful to realize that some of the nuttiest people were judges, lawyers, hospital administrators, and surgeons. The message was awesome. You can be a very responsible adult and still enjoy life. There's no need to kill off the inner child in the interest of productivity.

As Loretta LaRoche constantly reminds people, "You are going to die." This is one of the few facts of life that is absolutely certain. And the end often comes sooner than you'd like. While it's a truism that life is a journey rather than a destination, it's so easy to forget how to enjoy the trip. All that you can really count on is that you're alive right now, reading this entry. Why not make the most of your time here?

In the late 1980s, when a diagnosis of AIDS was a fairly certain death sentence, I told a group of AIDS patients at a mind/body skills group that none of us knows when the end of life will come. Although apparently healthy, I might have an accident on my way home and die before any of them. In fact, I had a serious head-on collision later that night. My seatbelt failed, and I almost lost my nose when it smashed against the steering wheel. Although it took two surgeries to repair my face, I'm grateful for the experience. Lying in the hospital with my nose in a sling, I realized how serious life had become. It was time to remember joy. So I quit my job and created a new life.

This week, give some thought to Loretta's funny tombstones. What might yours say if you died tomorrow? "Ate bean sprouts and went jogging; dead anyway"? or "Finished every item on the list and died totally pissed off"? Take a few minutes and write out a better one. Then do your best to live it.

I want mine to say, "She loved a lot, was kind and silly, was a friend you could count on, knew how to play, and did a reasonably good job even though she didn't return all her phone calls."

34. Try Power Whining

⧓⧓

One of the most common complaints that men have about women is that we complain too much. Some men are pretty good at it, too. But no matter what your gender is, complaining can compromise other people's inner peace as well as your own.

I once appeared on *Oprah* as the so-called expert on how people cope with life-threatening illness. It was a pleasure to be upstaged by a man with a debilitating neurological disease called ALS, or Lou Gehrig's disease. Confined to a wheelchair, he'd lost almost all function. Since he could no longer breathe on his own, a respirator breathed for him. Unable to eat, he was fed through a tube. Unable to speak, he could just barely move his lips. No problem. His wife and nurse lip-read. With their help, unbelievably enough, he had become a motivational speaker.

The man was a stunning, if somewhat daunting, inspiration. Compared to his dire circumstances, my usual complaints about busyness, fat thighs, and rude drivers paled to narcissistic insignificance. He had every right to be depressed and angry, and I'm sure he had his moments. But according to his loved ones, he was really and truly a teacher of peace. When Oprah asked how he kept his spirits up, he replied that we all have the same choice. We can have a pity party or a peaceful heart. He made a practice of choosing peace.

Every one of us is faced with the same choice, but those who choose whining over peace usually find allies in the process. Let's say that you're minding your own business, perhaps even feeling chipper. Then along comes someone trolling for sympathy, in person or on the telephone. They want you to come to a pity party. The opening gambit might go something like this: "You look (or sound) so tired. You do so much for everyone. Are you okay?"

The expected response is for you to heave a great big sigh and then to list all the things that are exhausting you, all the people who need your help, all the ingrates who fail to appreciate your true worth, and all the things that you'd rather be doing. Then the other person tries to outdo you.

"You think you're busy? I had to fly to Madagascar for a lunch meeting and then be back in time for my son's Pinewood Derby in Cub Scouts. I'm the den mother and had to make brownies. Since the kitchen floor was all scuffed from the new puppy that no one takes care of but me, I had to wax it before the parents brought their kids over. My husband slipped on it later when he was getting a glass of water to bring to bed. I drove him to the emergency room while he was shrieking with pain. Since there were four people with gunshot wounds ahead of him, it took hours for them to suture his leg and set his compound fracture. I didn't get to bed until three in the morning, and then had to get to work for an early breakfast meeting."

In no time at all, the two of you can work up a case of misery that would make a blues singer proud. Remember Linda Ronstadt's funny and doleful song "Poor, Poor Pitiful Me"? I like to play it when I'm in a funk because the parody is so evident that it jolts me into my right mind. The question is, why do perfectly sane people insist on making pity party a serious competitive sport? Obviously, the game can make you feel a little better in the short run because it provides support from other miserable people. And misery loves company. It's a coping strategy.

Mutual complaining is a form of what psychologists call *regressive coping*. When you're in the process of whining, you're moving backward in time, acting like a helpless child rather than a self-actualizing adult. The other whiner is supporting you in your regression, rather than challenging you to achieve self-awareness and growth. Healthy social support spawns authentic coping that challenges you to find greater meaning and opportunity in life. It encourages awareness and humor, and helps you develop new coping strategies while celebrating the ones that already work well.

Wacky wise woman Loretta LaRoche suggests that when

you want to whine, you might find a friend and do it right. Each of you gets two minutes to complain to your hearts' content without interruption. Hopefully you'll get everything off your chest, creating a parody of the pity party without taking it seriously. If you have another few minutes, each of you can then take a turn, listing everything that you're grateful for. That leaves you in a much better frame of mind.

This week, watch out for regressive coping. You can easily turn down invitations to complain by mentioning the things that are going well. Being busy can be a blessing. Try focusing on the positive whenever the desire to complain comes up. If you need to let off steam, put your hands on your hips while standing in front of a mirror, and power whine for two minutes. Pretty funny, aren't you?

35. Cultivate Gratitude

The attitude of gratitude is the culmination of all the strategies for inner peace. When you learn to manage your mind, take care of yourself, relate to others with compassion and kindness, and develop a mindful approach to life, gratitude will arise all by itself. In the meantime, you can practice it. A little run-in with a big German shepherd helped me do just that.

One clear winter's day, I decided to take a walk in the tiny Colorado wilderness town where we live. The sky was a shade of blue peculiar to the higher elevations of the Rockies. The early March sun poured like liquid gold through the limbs of tall spruce trees, creating dancing patterns of light in the delicate crystals of freshly fallen snow. Mountain peaks rose majestically in sculpted layers of purples, greens, and grays, piercing clouds that hung like fairy mist in the enchanted valleys below.

Marching resolutely down the road, I was all but blind to the extraordinary beauty. Attempting to relax before driving down the mountain to undergo a breast biopsy at the local hospital, I was reviewing the menu of calamitous medical possibilities that might materialize. As my mind slid into well-worn patterns of awfulizing, it gathered momentum. Not only might my body be in mortal danger, but life wasn't working so well in other ways either. Not only did the glass seem half-empty, but the remaining water appeared downright polluted. I felt overworked and burned out. What kind of crazy life had I managed to create, especially when I'm supposed to be some kind of role model for others? Guilt, fear, anger, and disappointment joined the cacophony of inner voices accompanying me down the road on my attempt at a mindful, relaxing walk.

I was rudely awakened from my toxic reverie by a searing pain in my hindquarters. Utterly focused on scary mental movies, I had been completely oblivious to the speedy approach of a large German shepherd who bounded up and bit me unceremoniously on the behind. My mental movie theater immediately began to run a feature film starring my bare buttocks being sutured in the Boulder Community Hospital emergency room, while I was simultaneously being injected with huge doses of tetanus toxoid and rabies vaccine. I would, no doubt, miss my biopsy and have to undergo that second round of medical torture on another day.

I reached down into my pants expecting to encounter a sticky mass of blood. My hand emerged perfectly clean. Energized by sudden hope, I slipped behind a bush and pulled my pants down. While a large red welt, framed by the impression of a perfect set of canine teeth, graced my derrière, the skin was unbroken. With a yelp of pure joy, I pulled up my pants and burst from the bushes with a whoop of gratitude. No emergency room. No tetanus shots. No slow death from rabies.

I could get to the biopsy on time. Lucky me.

Suddenly, the entire scene seemed hysterically funny. The dog was transformed from a nasty cur into a divine messenger. "Wake up, you silly human! Feel the sun on your face and the wind in your hair. You're alive and the world is beautiful. The mountains are magnificent, and the day is young. There are endless possibilities to experience and worlds to create." I was overwhelmed with gratitude for the gift of life. Every breath was precious, every tree a miracle. Peace settled around me like a down quilt.

Gratitude is like a gearshift that can move your mental mechanism from obsession to peacefulness, from rigidity to creativity, from fear to love. The ability to relax and be mindfully present in the moment comes naturally when you're grateful. One of the most delightful aspects of my Jewish heritage is the saying of Brachot—blessings or prayers of thanksgiving throughout the day. These are praises of God for creating a world of vast wonder. There is a blessing upon seeing a star or a rainbow. There is a blessing for the gifts of food, wine, and water. There's even a bathroom blessing for internal organs that function so well. I like to add impromptu blessings throughout the day. Thanks for German shepherds who teach us peace at the most unlikely times. Thanks, too, for a biopsy that was negative—one of the few instances where a negative turns out to be positive.

This week, when you find yourself awfulizing, try focusing on gratitude for all the things that are right. Years ago, I learned an exercise from the Benedictine monk, Brother David Steindl-Rast, author of the beautiful book, *Gratefulness, The Heart of Prayer*. He suggested that every night before bed, you say thanks for something that you've never thought about being grateful for before. It's easy for the first few weeks, but then you really have to think to come up with something new. If you continue the exercise (which takes almost no time, you'll be happy to realize) for a few months, you'll begin noticing things to be grateful for throughout the day, knowing that you'll need something new to be thankful for that night. This simple exercise makes you mindful and has the power to change your life.

36. Walk with a Positive Attitude

☙☘

There are many ways to develop awareness of your mind and feelings. This particular strategy takes advantage of an activity that most of us do every day: walking. But even folks in wheelchairs can relate to perambulating with a positive attitude.

While at a conference in Florida, I came upon a wonderful little book on walking meditations. It was an old favorite that had been lent out and lost track of, so I bought a new copy and headed out the door to read in the shade of a palm tree. "Peace is in every step," teaches gentle monk and author Thich Nhat Hanh. I planned to relish his wise, poetic words and then to practice slow, mindful walking.

A young girl of seven or eight was approaching the lobby as I was walking out. Dressed in pink capri pants, a T-shirt advertising Disney World, and a pair of white sneakers with ruffled socks, she wore a particularly radiant smile. Marching smartly along, her hands tucked under her armpits, she was flapping exuberant little wings in time to a singsong chant belted out with gusto: "Walk, walk, walk, walkety, walk, walk, walk," she sang over and over as she marched toward the door like a drum majorette.

Was I imagining it, or did she grace me with a conspiratorial glance? There *I* was, ready to read and study so that I might find peace and joy while walking. There *she* was, the perfect natural walking lesson. So I went to a secluded area behind the hotel to try her marching and singing technique. But I felt anything but peaceful. Standards of behavior change substantially between the ages of 7 and 55. I was waiting to be hauled off by the men in the white coats.

So I went for a more sedate stroll, with the idea of noticing how walking reflects our moods. A few people slouched by, looking tired and worn. One older couple, sunburned and carefree, held hands and skipped. Some people meandered along happy and alert, while others seemed preoccupied. A few appeared grim and determined, like spies on a mission. Many people were studies in busyness. Their shoulders were hunched up around their ears, and they walked leaning forward, as if leading with their heads would get them to their destination more quickly. That, I realized, was how I often walked myself. If the walk could talk, it would say, "Get out of my way! I'm busy, and I've got important things to do." There are friendlier and more peaceful walks.

Ever the inquiring biologist, I experimented with several different walking styles. The slouching, depressed walk made me feel . . . well, depressed. The busy, determined walk kindled anxiety. All of the undone to-do's bubbled up unbidden. How could I even think of relaxing on vacation? My attempt at measured steps and peaceful breathing, a Thich Nhat Hanh kind of walk suitable for the country, felt conspicuous and inauthentic on a city street. It was out of rhythm with the pace, and catching a glimpse of my reflection in a window, I appeared to be drugged. A naturally paced, curious walk where I was alert to the sights and sounds of the city was the most interesting and fun.

Research with seasoned actors who can make faces without feeling embarrassed or self-conscious shows that the expressions we make affect our mood. You're happier if you smile, sadder if you frown. Your body mobilizes the fight-or-flight response if your face shows fear or anger. If you add body posture and movement to the expression on your face, mood changes are even more pronounced. We know that the mind affects the body. But we often forget that the body affects the mind.

Why not make the time you spend walking each day a lesson in peace and relaxation instead of busyness and anxiety? Try making this "walking awareness week." Experiment by walking with curiosity, joy, sensuousness, or peace. Try the busy, get-out-of-my-way, boy-am-I-important walk. Smile coolly like the Queen of England, and walk down the street with consummate benevolence. Sneak down the street like James Bond, tracking Goldfinger. Notice how each type of walk affects you. You may also notice that people respond to you differently as you shift your walk. The key to this experiment in peace is awareness. Choose a positive walk and see how your mind and body respond.

37. Listen to Your Heart

❧❧

When I was little, my mother used to ask me if I would jump out the window just because my friends were doing it. The question made me mad. Her approach might have lacked finesse, but she was trying to teach me an important lesson about life. Learn to think for yourself and listen to your heart, or you're likely to get into trouble.

Sometimes listening to yourself is hard, particularly when your circle of friends has cherished opinions. In our group, the belief that when something is supposed to happen it will flow along smoothly is a strong one. Conversely, if something is *not* meant to happen, obstructions will arise to prevent it.

When my husband, Kurt, and I got married, things went anything but smoothly. We had to jump over several roadblocks on the way to the altar. The first one concerned the wedding invitations. We put them in a used manila envelope to keep them safe on the way to the post office. Instead of mailing them personally, I handed the big unsealed envelope to a postal worker and explained that individual letters were inside. That was the last glimpse we had of them. The helpful but confused man must have sealed the envelope. The whole batch was mysteriously delivered to the return address, where it laid unopened for months.

The postal service played a second major role in the apparent anti-nuptial conspiracy. A friend sent flowers to decorate our home where the wedding was to be held. They arrived on a Saturday afternoon, but since the long package was too large to fit in our rural mailbox, the letter carrier dropped off a notice to pick it up at the post office on Monday. Unfortunately, the wedding was on Sunday.

What's a woman to do? I called a friend to commiserate. "Don't get married," she yelped in evident distress. "Can't you see that this is a strong sign? Two signs, in fact! It's not meant to be. Please just call the whole thing off."

My husband-to-be was less than thrilled with her response. He opined, in the words of the great master of metaphor, Sigmund Freud, "Sometimes a cigar is just a cigar." And he was right. We had a wonderful wedding ceremony. Each of our friends performed a meaningful ritual to help celebrate and consecrate our marriage. One couple had actually called the chief of the Nanticoke Indians, the tribe from which some of my husband's ancestors hailed, and got a description of their traditional wedding customs. The prescribed ritual involved holding hands, wrist to wrist, so that we could feel each other's heart beating. It was a powerful metaphor for the intimacy that a good marriage creates. Like most marriages, our five-year union has had its challenges, but I'm grateful that I followed my heart and married a man who has helped bring out my love of life and sense of humor.

A few months after the wedding, Kurt and I left for a vacation to an island in British Columbia, off the west coast of Canada. Kurt, who's part Native American, wanted to visit a village of Klahoos Indians that had been repatriated to their tribal lands on the island. Unlike the United States government, which continues to oppress Indians and violate treaties, the Canadian government is more benevolent toward her First Nations people. They had given a grant to the Klahoos to carve a large ocean-going canoe as part of a program to restore pride in their cultural heritage.

Thousand-year-old cedar trees nearly wide enough to drive a car through created a woodland cathedral of deep silence and dappled light. As we approached, the rhythmic sound of hammer and chisel led us to a clearing where two men were at work. The head carver was a well-known native artist, a gentle and humble man with strong hands and a peaceful heart. He showed us the giant stump of the 600-year-old tree that had been felled to make the canoe. It was easily eight feet in diameter. Unfortunately, the middle had rotted out and the tree was hollow. The canoe would have to be very narrow, carved from less than half the diameter of the tree. He explained that this was the first of many problems they had encountered.

The canoe was a work of art in any case, elegant and sleek. But there was a large crack at one end, where it was broken almost in half and would have to be mended with wooden pegs. The inexperienced tree cutters had not only chosen a hollow tree, they had also neglected to make a soft bed of needles to cushion its fall, or to clear the area where the behemoth would land. The ancient cedar had fallen across a log and had practically snapped in two.

Only a few weeks remained to finish the canoe in time for a festive launch, long in the planning. A lot of work remained, and the carver had only one apprentice. We asked whether more people were coming to help. He calmly shook his head no. Carving is very difficult, painstaking work. Several men had given it a try, but only one stayed, he told us.

Things are not going so well here in the forest primeval, I thought glumly. If my friend who had counseled me to call off the wedding were here, she would probably pronounce the canoe a lost cause as well. I could almost hear her voice in my head: "When things don't flow, they aren't meant to be."

I turned to the wiry carver with his open smile and easy-going manner, thinking carefully about how to choose the right words. I hesitated, and then finally said, "You've had more than your share of problems with this canoe project, but you seem so positive and hopeful. I'm wondering if there's a cultural difference. When these kinds of problems crop up in my world, there are people who take the obstructions as a sign that the project isn't meant to be. What do you think?"

His wise eyes locked onto mine, and he smiled warmly, revealing a set of perfect white teeth. "Oh, obstructions are good signs, my friend. Good signs, indeed. This project is very blessed. The bigger the spirit that is trying to be born, the greater the troubles that it must overcome. This makes it stronger. And this canoe has a very big spirit. It is the rebirth of our clan's pride and our identity."

As the carver spoke of the canoe, I thought about my marriage. For a moment, I was overjoyed. The carver's interpretation of obstacles was much more positive than my friend's had been. Then I saw the truth. Whether I picked his explanation or hers, I still wasn't thinking for myself and listening to my own heart. I was giving my power away to someone else.

We live in a world of instant experts. They preach on talk shows and write for magazines. They tell us what to think and how to manage our lives. Eat this and you'll be thin and happy. Think that and you'll manifest the life of your dreams.

Be good and you'll never get sick. Follow the signs, and the angels will guide you.

In a busy world, it's tempting to believe that someone else has the answers. Sometimes they do, but even then, their answers may not be yours. This week, remember that *you* are the authority on your own life. You'll be more peaceful if you listen for the wisdom in other people's advice, then take what serves you and leave the rest. In the end, peace comes from knowing yourself . . . and trusting yourself to make decisions that serve life and love.

38. What, Me Meditate?

೫ ೯

In terms of strategies for managing the mind, meditation is like doing mental push-ups that strengthen the muscles of awareness and choice. While it's not a practice that most people are willing to adopt for life, even several weeks of meditation can help train your mind and change your attitudes. If you should decide to keep it up, the benefits for the body are just as positive. The majority of regular meditators, however, are most interested in the soul. In virtually every religious tradition, meditation is practiced as a way to reach divine union.

However, you don't have to be religious to meditate. One of my mentors and former colleagues, Harvard cardiologist Dr. Herbert Benson, realized in the 1960s that any repetitive mental activity that shuts down the mind's busy chatter elicits a physiological shift to peace. He called this the relaxation response. It is the body's natural balance to the fight-or-flight, or stress, response. Research on the relaxation response proves that even ten minutes a day can strengthen your immune system, improve sleep, lower blood pressure, help to prevent irregular heartbeat, lower levels of the stress hormone cortisol, decrease anxiety, and increase joy and peace. That's a big return for a few minutes of your time.

You may not think of yourself as a meditator, but everyone has done it. For example, when you're totally focused on balancing your checkbook, recording each number and doing the calculations, time seems to fly. Rather than thinking about other things, you're absorbed in the task. It can be a relaxing activity unless you're worried about your finances. Knitting has a similar effect. The repetitive movement of the needles and yarn quiets the mind and allows your naturally peaceful inner core to shine through. Perhaps that's why knitting has become so popular in our busy world.

But you can't whip out your knitting needles or your checkbook everywhere you go. The most portable focus for eliciting the relaxation response is in your mind. If you're religious, you can use a bit of scripture or song from your tradition as a repetitive mental focus. A Greek Orthodox patient of mine experienced profound peace whenever the "Kyrie Eleison," a hymn about the mercy of Jesus, was sung in church. I suggested that he begin his meditation by chanting it aloud a few times, letting peace fill him up. Then he chanted it silently for 10 or 15 minutes. Not only did this simple, pleasurable practice elicit the physiological benefits of the relaxation response, it was a communion with his Higher Power.

Bringing the mind to a single focus is called *concentration meditation*. If we were taught this skill in childhood, think how much more creative, productive, and peaceful we would be as adults. Focusing the mind isn't easy. It takes practice. But just like learning to play the piano or driving a car, it soon becomes second nature. Can you remember how difficult it was to keep everything straight when you learned how to drive? It was hard, but after a few weeks, things fell into place. The key to learning meditation is realizing that most people find it difficult at first. They aren't automatically delivered to a state of bliss—they might still be thinking about trivial matters such as what to eat for breakfast.

You might decide, for example, to concentrate on belly breathing as a form of meditation. Perhaps you're focused on noticing your belly expand on the in-breath and relax on the out-breath. Then a thought occurs: *This is so relaxing, why don't I get around to it more often?* One thought leads to others: *I'm so busy and stressed. I really need this. No one helps around the house. Am I the only one who can change a toilet paper roll?* Soon you're ruminating rather than meditating. The key is to notice your thinking as soon as possible, and then as gently as you can, let go and return to the repetitive mental focus.

Many people give up on trying to meditate when they find out how busy the mind is. Thoughts such as, *I'm no good at this; other people relax right away, but my mind is too busy,* can stop you in your tracks. Make no mistake about it. Thinking will continue. That's the nature of the mind. The goal of concentration meditation is not to *stop* the mind, but rather to learn a potent form of mental martial arts. When thoughts come (and they will), you have a choice. You can notice and let them go, or keep on thinking. In 10 or 15 minutes, you might have to bring your mind back to focus dozens of times. This strengthens the mental muscles of letting go. After just a few weeks of practice, you'll see that it's much easier to control your mind throughout the day. You've been in training.

With a little more practice, you'll discover a layer of mind deeper than your thoughts. Just as the surface of the ocean can be turbulent—although it's calm several feet below—so goes your mind. Meditation trains you to descend to the level of peace. It's another way of finding the eye of the storm.

One of the greatest benefits of meditation is awareness. If someone were to say, "I'll give you a penny for your thoughts," I'd wager that about half the time you couldn't really say what you were thinking. You were vacationing in Never-Never Land, that zoned-out state in which you miss your exit on the highway. That's the familiar mindless condition where the lights are on, but nobody's home. Meditation increases mindfulness so that you can experience more choice, freedom, and pleasure.

Mindfulness meditation is a tradition unto itself. Unlike concentration meditation, in which you keep bringing yourself back to a single focus, mindfulness meditation is about expanding your awareness to notice all that you can without judging it. If you feel cool, for example, the idea is to avoid thinking of that as bad or good, which immediately changes the experience. Instead, you simply notice what the sensation of coolness is like. My favorite mindfulness meditation is eating a piece of chocolate cake with full attention. You might like to try it.

My colleague Dr. Jon Kabat-Zinn, director of the Center for Mindfulness in Medicine, Health Care, and Society at the University of Massachusetts Medical School, does an exercise in which every participant gets two raisins. They eat them mindfully, savoring the smell, the texture, and the sensation of saliva filling the mouth that makes the taste extraordinary. Mindfulness meditation can expand the world and make even the most mundane activity an adventure. You might enjoy Dr. Kabat-Zinn's book on mindfulness, *Wherever You Go, There You Are*.

There are as many ways to meditate as there are human beings. What works for one person may leave another cold. Concentration meditation is straightforward and can be learned from a book. Mindfulness meditation is more easily learned with a teacher. Fortunately, Dr. Kabat-Zinn's Stress Reduction and Relaxation programs are available at several hundred hospitals across the country. If you want to learn how to meditate, or even if you're an experienced meditator who wants to try different techniques, consult the Resources section of this book for a listing of my many meditation tapes available through Hay House.

This week, give meditation a try. If you're a beginner, start slowly. Five minutes is enough. If you like it, you can increase the length as you see fit. Research shows that 10 to 20 minutes, four or five times a week, is enough to create and sustain the physiological and psychological benefits of the practice. Keep this advice firmly in mind: *The only definition of a good meditation is one that you did.* The goal is not to experience peace during the practice session. The goal is to train the mind so that gradually you will feel more peace, awareness, and choice at all times. If the whole five minutes seems to consist of hauling your mind back from its reveries, then rejoice. You got a lot of practice in mental martial arts.

Like all habits, meditation takes commitment. It's best to meditate at the same time and in the same place each day. If you've created a place of refuge in your home, meditate there. On the other hand, one of my patients used to do it in her car during her lunch break at work, since she had small children at home. My friend Janet takes her shower and then meditates while her hair is drying. When she's done, it's at the perfect degree of dampness for blow-drying. I like to meditate before bed, but some people find that this revives them and interferes with sleep. The most important thing is to find a time that works for you . . . and to be consistent about the practice.

✑ ✑ ✑

PART V

Strategies for Developing Compassion, Kindness, and Clear Communication

39. Build Your Heart Intelligence

The Dalai Lama repeatedly says that his religion is kindness. I had the opportunity to interview His Holiness about health and healing in 1989 as part of an international conference. I knew that he was a highly learned man, and was told to ask questions about science and medicine that Buddhist knowledge might give us new insights about. I was nervous. *Terrified* might be a better word. What if I made a fool of myself or violated some important protocol? But fear evaporated as soon as he entered the room. His gentle eyes and thousand-watt smile penetrated the clouds of worry and touched my peaceful center. In his presence, I felt absolutely at home. I could feel his respect, attention, and love for me— a stranger. I vowed then and there to extend the respect and kindness that I felt from him to others.

His Holiness often says that we neglect the importance of affection. While we continue to learn about the brain and the intellect, we ignore the heart. The result is that our technological and scientific know-how becomes destructive. We have mind intelligence, but we lack the intelligence of the heart. We can send a rocket to the moon, yet we step over a homeless person on our own block right down here on planet Earth.

I live in the affluent town of Boulder, Colorado. But even here, there are battered wives, addicts, mentally ill folks, and families down on their luck. One day I was walking along our beautiful outdoor pedestrian mall when a bearded, somewhat ragged beggar about my age approached. Judgment rushed up, and I found myself thinking, *Why doesn't he just get a job?* Then I remembered His Holiness, and how he had acknowledged and respected me. So, instead of rushing off to do my errands, I decided to take a few minutes and ask the beggar what turn his life had taken to bring him here, panhandling for change on a bitter winter's day.

His name was "John." We sat down on a bench, and he told me about signing up to go to Vietnam in the 1960s. John was 18 then, brave and idealistic. He wanted to serve his country. Most of his battalion was killed in a bloody ambush, his best friend's lifeblood pulsing out on the jungle floor as John cradled his head in his arms and wept.

There was a long silence. As a therapist, I was thinking about how difficult it is to recover from such an unholy tragedy, how the interior horror movies can replay endlessly and rob a person of life. We call this nightmare post-traumatic stress disorder. Some of the brain chemistry involved is understood, but there's still a long way to go in treating it.

Where had he gone for treatment? I wondered aloud. John was still in treatment off and on, I learned, but it hadn't helped much. He lived alone, camping like a nomad in the Indian Peaks Wilderness, and coming to town very rarely. Today was one of those days, and he was panhandling for money to buy a few necessities to sustain his spare life. He looked at me with a wry smile, vestiges of a handsome young face still peeking out from the layers of fatigue, horror, and heartbreak that had plagued him for 35 years. In that moment, I saw my two sons, Justin and Andrei. This man, too, was some mother's son.

For a moment, we held hands and looked into one another's eyes, just two human beings sitting together on a bench. What could I say? "I'm so sorry. So very sorry." In that small moment when two hearts touched, we shared the sacrament of peace.

I never saw John on the mall again, but he's still with me. Sometimes when I get caught up in complaining about being too busy, I think of his soft brown eyes and what they've seen. In that moment of compassion, of heart intelligence, gratitude wells up. I have a life. There is a precious opportunity to learn and love, to give and receive. I've had my share of pain, but John has had *more* than his share. It makes me humble and puts my problems in perspective. Compassion is the great equalizer. I don't pity John. As writer Stephen Levine comments, pity is when your *fear* touches another person's suffering, but compassion is when your *love* touches another person's suffering. Pity leaves you raw and empty. Compassion leaves you full and peaceful.

Devote this week to building up your heart intelligence. You don't have to sit down with every suffering person and ask about their story. It's enough to know that they *have* a story. For the most part, they've faced their life in the best and bravest way they could, given their history and circumstances. They are deserving of your kindness and respect.

As you go about your business and busyness this week, think about each person you see during the day as a human being just like yourself, trying to find peace and happiness just like you are. When your heart opens even a little, your peaceful core shines out, your body and mind relax, and compassion helps you calm down and come home to yourself.

40. Be a Source of Kindness

I was once in a head-on collision and sustained a serious head injury. Slumped over the wheel and still dazed, I was in the process of trying to assess the extent of the injuries. The accident occurred in an impoverished section of Boston, known for drive-by shootings and robberies. It should also be known as a place of kindness.

The driver's side door creaked open, and there stood a stranger who had stopped her car to help. This African-American woman of indeterminate age knelt by my side and reached out a big warm hand to touch my hair. She flinched when she saw the blood on my crushed face and then reached for my hand instead. "Don't you worry 'bout nothin', honey. You gonna be *all* right. Help is on the way, and I be right here. I ain't goin' nowhere."

I can still hear those comforting words, exactly as she said them. I can still feel her kind voice wrapping around me like a cocoon to keep out the terror. She waited with me until an ambulance arrived. Even then, this stranger, who for a few brief moments had become the center of the world, stayed by my side until the gurney was loaded and the ambulance door slammed shut.

I attribute the fact that I still have a nose—although it was nearly destroyed in the accident—to that woman's simple act of kindness. Her comforting touch and reassuring words must have kept my blood pressure down, minimizing damage to the tissues. I think about her from time to time and wish that I could thank her. But that wish is more for me than for her. Kindness is its own reward. It gladdens the heart of the giver. According to the First Law of Spiritual Mathematics (one of my little unofficial rules for life), any kindness given is returned tenfold.

If you think about it, you may find that a certain act of kindness was a watershed moment in your life, or at least a re-affirmation of your faith. My friend Kathleen flew across the country to care for a friend's toddler while his mother took a trip. Kathleen had taken the little boy out to breakfast, and then saved the uneaten portion of his meal in a cardboard take-out box that she placed in the basket of his stroller. Their walk took them into a poor section of Baltimore, where Kathleen wanted to see a famous Basilica. En route, she stopped to offer the child a few more bites of breakfast from the box. A homeless woman approached them and told Kathleen that if she wanted a hot meal for the child, there was a good place right down the street.

The concern of the homeless woman was so touching that it brought Kathleen to tears, although she did wonder if she really resembled a bag lady. But there, for the grace of God, could go any one of us. Even when we have nothing material to give, kindness is bread for the journey. Whatever Kathleen had hoped to find in the Basilica, she found in the streets instead. For when are we closer to God than when we care for one another?

Several years ago, a little book called *Random Acts of Kindness* became a surprise best-seller. It suggested that we might spread some joy through small kindnesses—such as feeding parking meters that are about to expire, or paying the toll for the car behind us. I was once a recipient of the latter act. It was a bit of a shock in these rude times when road rage is a far more common phenomenon.

The key to kindness is to recognize that other people are just like you. They have hopes and fears, joys and sorrows, just like you do. In this busy world, it's easy to see people as *roles* rather than as human beings. Service people such as waiters and waitresses, police and letter carriers, road crews and garbage collectors, often fail to get their due.

My son Justin is a restaurant manager, and he's waited his share of tables. He's full of stories about kind and unkind customers. Once he got a $50 tip on a $100 tab. Justin is a very polite, engaging, knowledgeable, and helpful young man, and the customer appreciated him. The appreciation was actually more important than the tip, although he was very happy to get that, too! On the other hand, he's also been tipped a dollar on a $100 check. Apparently those customers thought that their dinner was expensive enough. They forgot that Justin was a human being, too, trying to make a living and pay his bills.

Last Christmas we tipped the trash collector, letter carrier, and road maintenance crew that's responsible for keeping our dirt road passable, graded, and plowed. It was a surprise to receive thank-you notes from each one. Even more surprising was the fact that they use most of their Christmas tips to buy presents for needy children.

This week, pay attention to kindness given and received. As busy as you are, take the time to write a thank-you note when someone has been kind to you. Make it personal so that they know how their thoughtfulness made a difference. Tell people when they've done a good job. Let your loved ones know that they're wonderful—not because of anything they *did*, but just because they *are*. You might also pull off a few random acts of kindness. They really are fun. If your act is directed to someone you know, do it anonymously. Having a favorite dessert materialize on your desk is a delicious mystery. It restores the soul as well as the body.

41. Practice Forgiveness

❧❧

A *Time* magazine cover story published in the early 1990s called forgiveness a clever strategy for a person or a nation to follow because forgiveness sets the forgiver free. My dear friend Robin Casarjian, author of *Forgiveness: A Bold Choice for a Peaceful Heart,* usually begins her teachings with an invitation: "Reach into your head and pull out all your opinions about forgiveness. Put them under your chair. If you still want them when we're through talking, you can just reach down and put them back in." I extend that same invitation to you now.

I was in Germany several years ago, teaching about forgiveness as part of a workshop on health and healing. Since I'm Jewish, and several family members had perished in Auschwitz, I took a close look at my feelings before the workshop. Was I still holding on to any anger and blame about the Holocaust? If so, I felt that it would be impossible to teach forgiveness to my German brothers and sisters. Since I felt free of resentment, it felt right to go ahead.

Some of the participants were children of Nazis. Theirs was a heavy load as they struggled to understand the behavior of their parents and break free from the chains of the past. During the workshop, we discussed what forgiveness is *not* so that we could better grasp what it *is*. It is *not* about condoning bad behavior. You can forgive the person who stole from you while testifying against them in court. Nor is it about setting conditions for redemption. Forgiveness is an understanding of the person as they are, rather than a stick to beat them into shape. Forgiveness is *not* about any particular behavior. You can forgive an abusive parent without ever going home again, or alternatively, you may start to show up for Sunday dinners. And most important, forgiveness is not something you do *for* another person. It is about setting yourself free and finding peace. The mercy you give is to *yourself*.

We joined together in an exercise of imagination that I learned from Robin many years ago. After centering in the breath, I invited the participants to imagine that they were in a safe and sacred place where others could enter only with their permission. They then imagined asking a person that they wanted to forgive—or a person that they hoped might forgive them—into their sanctuary. There they had a heart-to-heart talk. The experience of expressing how you feel, and then listening for the response, can be very moving. When I facilitate this kind of experience in workshops, I always warn the women that it's going to be a bad mascara day.

In the ladies' room after the exercise, a woman approached me. She talked about having dinner the previous evening with the most courageous, compassionate man she knew. I couldn't disguise the sudden look of judgment that distorted my features when she told me that he had been one of the doctors who conducted medical experiments in the concentration camps. Visions of the monster Mengele danced in front of my eyes. Suddenly, the Holocaust felt personal again. I knew at that moment that in spite of the belief that I'd forgiven the Nazis, there were still cords of judgment binding me to the past.

The doctor's assignment was to inject children with a toxin, and then catalog the damage that it did to the organs of the body. They had to be kept in the infirmary for the duration of the experiment, under close observation. He gathered as many children as the building could possibly hold. But instead of injecting poison, he administered a harmless salt solution. In that way, he kept the children safe. They were clothed, fed, and treated tenderly. Every child in his care lived to be liberated. At any time during the years in which he protected these little ones, his treason might have been discovered. He had the courage to act with love, even though his life was at stake.

I had never thought much about the unknown heroes of the Holocaust. There must have been a lot of them. Neither had I thought about how many German people of good heart had suffered during those dark times. The woman's story, and the understanding it engendered, helped me become more compassionate. That is the magic of forgiveness. It can turn wounds into wisdom and make closed hearts open. It can replace tolerance with love.

On the same trip to Germany, I visited Dachau, a former concentration camp on the outskirts of Munich. It is now a museum. By some force of grace, it happened to be All Soul's Day, the European equivalent of Halloween. But while Americans are largely ignorant of the meaning of this holy day, Europeans remember that it's a time to visit the dead. German parents brought their children to Dachau, leaving stone cairns topped with red votive candles. The barracks, dirt roads, work houses, and ovens had all been transformed to altars of reconciliation and forgiveness.

Several religious groups have built shrines at Dachau. Because it was nearing dark, I had only enough time to visit the Jewish shrine. It's crafted to create an experience of reflection, and, hopefully, forgiveness. The entrance is a metal fence made to look like barbed wire. You must get down on all fours to enter, crawling through a dark tunnel like a birth canal. The tunnel leads into a circular room, like a womb. A hole at the top of the round ceiling is the only source of light.

A single candle burns in the shrine perpetually, and I found myself reflecting on its symbolism of life, hope, and renewal. Other than the eternal light, there is only one other object in the shrine: A plaque from the people of the town hangs on the spare, stone wall. It expresses heartfelt regret. How could this Holocaust have been allowed to happen? Sitting on my haunches in the shadows, I thought about the Nazi doctor who had saved so many Jewish children. Then I thought about all the people who might have liked to stop the slaughter but felt powerless. Their grief lingered like a vapor in that holy place. I understood. And I wept for them. If I had brought a votive candle, I would have made a cairn of stones and lit a candle for them. They, too, were victims.

As I crawled back out of the shrine into the gathering darkness, I felt reborn. I had come to Germany to teach forgiveness, and it was I who had learned to forgive. A fellow Jew by the name of Jesus spoke truly when he told his followers not to judge so that they themselves would not be judged. I have found his words to be true. As we learn to let go of judgment, which is another way of defining forgiveness, we are less likely to judge ourselves. And it is self-judgment that is the most bitter pill of all. Everyone makes mistakes, but it's when we learn from them that they become their own redemption. In forgiving ourselves for what we've done, we can celebrate what we've become.

This week, make a fearless inventory of your regrets and

resentments. Wherever possible, without hurting anyone, make amends. That is the beginning of self-forgiveness. And as Robin always says, be gentle with yourself. Forgiveness may take time. You won't complete it in a week. You may not even complete it in a lifetime. But it's the most worthwhile pursuit for inner peace. As you seek to understand your own pain and limitations, and the pain of those who have hurt you, you'll develop compassion. That's the highest purpose of your enemies. They are the most relentless teachers of the heart.

42. Judge Not

How true it is that if we could walk a mile in another person's shoes, judgment would fall away as understanding dawned. Unless they have serious emotional wounds, most people do the best they can, even though they make mistakes in the process of learning. But when the opportunity to understand someone is lacking, The Judge often makes an unpleasant and aggravating appearance.

When I was in my late 30s, a colleague was ostensibly trying to be helpful. He told me that I was naturally beautiful and didn't need makeup and nice clothes to be attractive. This was no come-on. His implication was that I was vain, shallow, and placed too much value on appearance because of some deepseated insecurity. I felt patronized and humiliated. Yet the vulnerable part of me believed him. Although I was hardly a Cosmo Girl, just kind of tastefully offbeat, I wondered whether it was a character flaw to want to look nice. I considered a return to younger years, when I was a crunchy-granola type of gal in Earth Shoes, unshaven legs, and couture straight from the Goodwill bin. Giving the matter serious thought, I finally decided to ignore my colleague's judgment and dress to please myself.

You might be wondering why that incident affected me so deeply. Who cares what other people think? Unfortunately, most of us do. The need to be acknowledged, respected, and loved is a survival issue. Our brains are hard-wired for approval because as infants, to be rejected is to be dead. It's easy to appreciate that we would have more inner peace if we were immune to praise and blame, as the ancient sages admonish us. But most of us are not.

Dr. Daniel Amen, a psychiatrist who studies how our brain chemistry affects behavior, has some good advice. He calls it the 18/40/60 rule. At 18, you care very much what other people think of you; at 40, you don't give a damn what they're thinking; and at 60, you realize that no one was thinking about you anyway. Dr. Amen's rule is wise, but we would be wiser and more peaceful still if we developed the wisdom of 60 in our younger years. We are not the center of other people's universes. Their role is not to judge, nor ours to obey. Inner peace requires us to develop the authority to direct our own lives, and the respect to allow other people to live theirs.

It helps to realize that judgments are often projections of something that we don't want to acknowledge about ourselves. Instead, we see that quality in the people around us. Restless people tend to notice impatience. Helpless people are prone to cast others in the role of victim. Angry people see rage all around them. Frightened people are experts on other people's fear and insecurity. Perhaps the colleague who was so concerned with my wardrobe was wrestling with his own unexpressed need to be special and to be noticed. In his desire to be humble and spiritual, he may have projected his fear of flamboyance onto me.

There is an old story about a man who's looking for a place to live where the people will be nicer than they are in his current neighborhood. When he asks a stranger in a new part of town what the people are like there, the stranger shakes his head and replies, "They're exactly like the people where *you* live."

Whether you move, change jobs, or look for a new mate, you're likely to experience some of the same irritations that you did in the previous circumstance. What bothers us about other people is often a reflection of our own shadow, the disowned parts of our personality that we judge and try to hide out of shame. Like our physical shadow, it follows us faithfully. It will work to our detriment until we're ready to see it, heal it, and forgive it.

By understanding other people's shadows, you become less vulnerable to their opinions. When you recognize that a criticism may be more about your critic than you, it's easier to let it pass, rather than taking it to heart. By understanding your own shadow, you're less likely to judge others unkindly. This week, notice the way that you respond to judgment and criticism, as well as your tendency to judge. You might try this tip that I learned from author, speaker, and wise guide, Ram Dass, many years ago. When you catch yourself grumbling about someone else, own the projection and say, "And I am that, too."

43. Guard Against Gossip

During the 1980s, when an epidemic of false accusations of child molestation by day-care workers turned into an ugly witch-hunt, our nation got firsthand experience in the damage that gossip can do. Rumors spread like wildfire within communities, and as they often do, the stories got embellished and distorted as they passed from person to person.

If you played "Whisper Down the Lane" as a child, you can probably recall how the simplest message lost its meaning as it was passed on down the line. The result was often wildly comical. But in real life, such distortions aren't funny at all. Scandal sticks to people who are subsequently found blameless and publicly exonerated. They are irreparably harmed through gossip.

Once you hear something damaging, or even mildly titillating about someone, it's hard to get it out of your mind. The nursery rhyme, "Sticks and stones can break my bones, but words can never hurt me," gives the wrong message to children. In actuality, broken bones mend soon enough, but reputations are much slower to heal.

I have a friend who's generally a kind and empathetic person, but she has an unfortunate addiction to gossip. She has the bad habit of trading information about one person for intimacy with the next. People soon realize that about her, and as a result, she has a large network of superficial friends, but few close ones since she can't be trusted. If a person regales you with intimate details of their other friends' lives, you can be sure that they're betraying your confidences in the same way. In Yiddish, such gossips are called *yentas*.

There's a story about three women who have played cards together every Saturday for 30 years. One day Martha says to her friends, "We've been together a long time, girls, so I'm going to tell you my darkest secret. I'm a nymphomaniac. But don't worry, your husbands are safe around me."

Emboldened by the honesty, June speaks next. "Since we're telling the truth, which is a great relief, I'm an undercover agent for the FBI."

"Thank you so much, girls," says Sarah. "My secret is that I'm a *yenta*. Sorry to break this up, but I've gotta run. I have some important phone calls to make."

All religions include an ethical prohibition against gossip. In Buddhism, it's one of the practices called "right speech," and one of the cornerstones of respect and compassion. Unfortunately, we live in a culture where right speech is a lost art.

Titillation and trash talk are common entertainment. From movie stars to politicians, we're inundated with the goriest and most intimate details of people's private lives. The more demeaning and degrading, the better. When Linda Tripp betrayed the confidence of her friend Monica Lewinsky, most people found her behavior reprehensible. It was a shocking betrayal that made Tripp the sorriest of the characters in the practically endless presidential sex scandal.

The sacrament of friendship depends upon being safe to open your heart fully and know that it will be protected. Good friends are a tree of shelter in hard times, and a source of joy and growth. They are the ground out of which inner peace grows. Having a confidante that you can trust with your hopes and fears, who loves you even after they've heard your darkest secrets, is a special grace. The ability to confide your secrets not only reduces anxiety and stress, it also helps protect you against heart disease, strengthens immunity, and aids the body's fight against cancer.

For this entire week, deepen your capacity for friendship by guarding against gossip in any form. Practice right speech. As your grandmother might have told you, if you don't have something nice to say about someone, say nothing at all. When another person begins to tell you more than you think you should know about someone else's business, let them know that you would rather not hear it. Every human being deserves the kindness and respect to be seen for who they are . . . rather than for who other people *think* they are.

44. Tap in to the Power of Your Authentic Self

❧❧

It's popular to talk about one's authentic self. The problem lies in figuring out what that is, since each of us has many selves. I am a mother and a wife, a writer and a speaker, a scientist and a psychologist, a compassionate person and a good friend. On the negative side of the ledger, I possess an array of alter-egos—false selves—that can emerge when I'm upset, depressed, afraid, or overtired. There's the martyr and the perfectionist, the whiner and the people-pleaser, the critic and the boss. Then there's Chicken Little, Queen of Pessimism, who likes to insist that the sky is falling. Which one of these characters is my authentic self? Or as the host on the old television program *To Tell the Truth* used to say, "Will the *real* Joan Borysenko please stand up!"

I learned a profound lesson about the authentic self at the Miraval Spa in Tucson, Arizona. In the winter of 2001, my friend Cheryl Richardson and I gave our first annual *Take Time for Your Life* retreat for a group of about 70 men and women in that beautiful desert setting. Afternoons were free to take advantage of Miraval's exceptional programs. Several members of our group raved about something called the Equine Experience. The horses, they said, were like mirrors that showed you who you really were. It was the experience of a lifetime for some people. Intrigued, Cheryl and I—along with our husbands—signed up.

The wrangler in charge was Wyatt Webb. He explained that our first task would be to clean out the hooves of the horse assigned to us. I found myself drifting into disappointment. During our 30s, my husband and I had two spunky mares, Quana the Quarterhorse and Mia the Arabian. I had picked the dirt and gravel out of plenty of hooves during those years, and couldn't imagine how the experience was about to shed any new light on my personality. But as Wyatt talked about how horses respond to our energy, mirroring our emotions and intentions, it was clear that he was a very wise man. I let go of judgment, eager to see what would unfold.

Whatever happened during the grooming, Wyatt warned

us not to make up any stories about our horse. If it seemed obstinate and refused to lift its hooves for cleaning, it wasn't being stubborn. Rather, *we* were not coming from our authentic selves. I still wasn't sure what that elusive self might be. We were dispatched with our hoof picks, some safety information, and this sage advice: "If what you're doing isn't working, try something else. If that doesn't work, ask for help."

I approached the horse with three parts confidence and two parts anxiety. It had been 20 years since I'd wielded a hoof pick, but when the horse dutifully lifted each back hoof for cleaning, I felt that I was on a roll. However, the front hooves turned out to be another story. I pinched the tendon as instructed to cue the horse to lift his left leg. Nothing doing. I pinched a little harder. Still nothing. Trying to look nonchalant, I walked around to the other side of the horse and repeated the whole drill again to no avail. So I called for help.

A wrangler by the name of John sauntered over. He's an amazing man who understands both horses and people. "How are you feeling?" he asked benignly.

"A little frustrated," I volunteered. Having once owned horses, I thought that I should have done better. And what if I was the only one who couldn't get the task done? How humiliating that would be.

In two minutes flat, John pointed out several of my false selves. The perfectionist thought that having kept horses 20 years ago should have qualified me as an expert today. The people-pleaser was very concerned about doing things right so that other people would think well of me. The horse, John assured me, couldn't give two hoots about those imposter selves and the palpable anxiety they generated. Horses are very sensitive to energy. They respond to peaceful clarity of intention. The emotional turmoil I was generating was not a clear form of communication.

John picked up a stick and drew a line in the dirt. "This is the Rio Grande River," he said. "On one side are your false selves—Joan the perfectionist, and Joan the people-pleaser. On the other side is the real Joan. That's the only one this horse will respond to."

John walked off to help another person, and I thought about how I could cross that river and be the Joan who was clear, peaceful, and present. I took a few deep breaths and decided that love was a good way to come into the moment. The horse and I might communicate better if I showed him some affection. So I nuzzled his rubbery lips and scratched behind his ears. I stroked his withers (the ridge between the shoulder bones) and whispered to him reassuringly. Then I tried to lift a hoof. It didn't budge. It felt like his leg had grown roots that extended to the center of the earth. Lover boy was glued to the spot.

More help was needed. A trim and smiling wrangler by the name of Ellen came over next. She had obviously been watching this little spectacle, and to the best of my recollection said something like this: "So, Joan, are you used to getting what you want by schmoozing?" She was so on-target that I burst out laughing while nodding my assent. "You can't schmooze a horse," she continued. "They don't care. They will only respond to your clear intention. Back off and take four or five deep breaths. Center yourself. Think clearly about what you want the horse to do, and then go over there and lift up his leg."

Understanding was beginning to dawn. I stepped back and took several belly breaths, searching for that inner center of peace. There are no false selves there. The people-pleaser, the perfectionist, and the rest of the cast of characters live on the other side of the river. *All I want is for the horse to lift his leg,* I thought. My intention was clear. All was calm on the Western front. I walked over to my four-legged teacher, lifted his leg, and cleaned that hoof. Like life, it was simple, but it had not initially been so.

Following the hoof cleaning, we had to lead our horses around the arena. This time I knew what to do, and I knew what the horse had to do. He knew that I knew, and we were in perfect communication. I was smiling like the Cheshire cat as a result of this little victory, knowing that the wisdom of how to take charge from my authentic self would serve me well in other areas of my life.

A few weeks later, while on another business trip, the zipper on my suitcase got stuck. I struggled with it, pulling and tugging. I was beginning to think that I would have to stuff all my belongings into a pillow case to complete the trip. A parade of false selves began to walk through my mental landscape. The perfectionist scolded me, pointing out that I should have taken different luggage. After all, I'd known that the zipper needed repair. The people-pleaser was concerned that I would look stupid, not to mention unprofessional, lugging my stuff around in a pillow case. The victim began to feel sorry for herself, stuck in a hotel room with an evil suitcase. This wouldn't do.

So I pretended that the zipper was the horse back at Miraval. I backed up, centered myself with several belly breaths, and thought about what my intention was. The zipper needed to let go and unzip. Remarkably, it did just that.

This week, notice the way that you approach your communications with people, animals, and even inanimate objects such as zippers. Are you clear about what your intention is? If things don't go your way, what false selves start speaking in your head? Take a few deep breaths and step into your authentic self rather than letting a false self run off with your peace and power. Find your center, and be clear about what you're communicating. Horses and other animals are not alone in their ability to pick up your energy. People do it, too. When your outer words and actions match what you're feeling inside, your energy is powerful and coherent. You can work wonders in a state of peaceful clarity.

45. Be a Good Listener

🜲🜲

One of the greatest gifts you can give to another person is listening. That simple act of kindness affords them the opportunity to share their thoughts and feelings. That's an important part of how we learn more about ourselves and develop a stronger sense of self. The bedrock of emotional health is the loving attention of our caregivers when we're babies. Infants in foundling homes whose needs for food and shelter are met, but whose feelings and verbalizations are not responded to, often develop failure-to-thrive syndrome. They become physically stunted and emotionally hardened.

But our need to be mirrored and responded to by other people doesn't end with childhood. It's a powerful emotional drive. Even as adults, being able to talk things through affects our bodies as well as our minds. An interesting study performed by psychologist James Pennebaker at Southern Methodist University showed that when people express their feelings to a shower curtain, their immune systems grow stronger. If talking to a silent plastic sheet provides so much benefit, just think of the impact that a live, loving listener can make.

When I was training to be a therapist, we had to do a fascinating exercise in pairs. One student played the role of the client, the other of the therapist. The client had to speak for 20 minutes. The therapist's job was to listen intently, without interrupting. Whenever we had the urge to say something, we were instructed to ask ourselves what was behind the impulse to talk. Did we want to make an empathetic comment, give advice, share an insight, or get clarification or further information?

The class noticed that the urge to interrupt often stemmed from the desire to reassure the speaker that we were interested.

Other times we just wanted to hear ourselves talk, or say something to appear smart and competent. Or perhaps we needed to relieve our own anxiety. That, of course, is not the role of a therapist. Overall, we concluded, most of the impulses to interrupt the client were better nipped in the bud.

The experience of being listened to without interruption was also a real eye-opener. My classmates reported almost unanimously that they felt accepted and understood by the silent listener. Because they had been allowed to keep talking, deep and often surprising insights had the chance to emerge. Without being cut off or redirected, a lot of us tapped in to a level of feeling and perception that was rare and valuable. Not a single person felt discounted by the lack of verbal response. In fact, we felt singularly appreciated.

Listening is a powerful form of communication. While the mouth is still, the heart can speak volumes about how much you care. I learned that lesson again when I sat with dying people. At first, I felt like I was supposed to say something comforting or wise. Sometimes I chattered just to relieve my own anxiety. Finally, I realized that just sitting with someone silently—even when they weren't talking—was still a form of listening. In your silent watchfulness, you become a safe space, one of love's most profound expressions.

Listening is an uncommon skill in our busy world. I recall an insightful cartoon that showed mourners at a funeral. The caption read something like: "So sorry for your loss; now back to my own problems." I've been guilty of that kind of self-absorption many times. And the busier I get, the more I need to guard against it. Several times while writing this book, feeling pressed to make the deadline, I caught myself turning back to the computer—just like an iron filing is drawn to a magnet—when someone wanted to talk.

While we can't be expected to drop everything we're doing and listen to whoever asks for our attention, we can give them the courtesy of telling them when we'll be available. That's a much kinder response than pretending to listen while continuing to read the paper, work at the computer, or watch television. Everyone occasionally responds with a distracted "uh-huh" when they're not really listening but making a habit of doing so discounts and dishonors people. When my husband, Kurt, complains that I'm not listening, I take the feedback seriously because I know that my behavior will ultimately take its toll on our love.

This week, concentrate on being a good listener for other people so that they can be themselves. When they've expressed themselves fully, try asking questions that draw them out a little more. How did they feel when the boss started talking about layoffs? What else was going through their minds? When you ask questions that stimulate further thought and emotional expression, you'll eventually find yourself on sacred ground. Both of you will have insights that are surprising—those that neither of you could have had alone. That's the magic of listening.

46. Communicate Honestly

༈ ༈

Many years ago, a physician whom I worked with decided to try a truth experiment in which any little embellishments or evasions were off-limits. He and his wife had made a deal to try it as a way of improving communication and building intimacy. The commitment to truth ended up having far-reaching effects on all of his relationships.

"Jack" had previously been fond of hyperbole and evasion. He was a funny guy, but used humor to keep his distance. A question such as, "How is your research going?" might have been answered with, "Tremendous. We're sure to get the Nobel

Prize." The response actually contained no useful information. It was a pleasant form of discounting the person who had posed the question.

Because of the truth experiment, Jack became precise and thoughtful. He'd answer that same question: "Well, a little slower than I'd like, really. Yesterday all of our gels collapsed and we can't figure out why. I'm feeling really frustrated. But overall, the results are encouraging. We're getting a much better idea about how calcium channels work. By the time that the grant renewal is due in February, I think we'll have enough data to write a strong one." This kind of answer honors the question, reveals important information about Jack's feelings and the progress of his research, and creates intimacy. Someone once defined *intimacy* as "into me you see." Jack started to let us do just that.

Little by little, the research team got to know him and genuinely like him. Before, Jack had been a remote, if pleasant, colleague who many of us had learned to ignore. One day he stopped me in the hall, looking pensive. I thought that I detected a little coolness, so I asked if he was annoyed with me for some reason. His head started to shake in denial. Then he straightened up and looked me in the eye. Jack was uncomfortable, but he was going to be honest anyway. "Actually, I am annoyed," he said. "You keep passing me without saying hello, and that makes me feel like I don't matter."

That was a surprise. I didn't think he would care. Furthermore, rushing from one task to the next, I'm the sort of person who stays very focused. I probably wouldn't have noticed a rhinoceros in the hall. When I explained that, Jack was relieved. For the two years that we had known one another, he had assumed that I didn't like him.

Then we got deeper into conversation. I admitted that while I always enjoyed his humor, until recently I didn't really know who he was, and I had felt a little bit uncomfortable around him. In that moment, two important things happened. First, we made a step toward friendship. Second, I became aware that my habit of intense focus could be as alienating as his habit of discounting through humor. I began to make a conscious effort to say hello to people, and all of my work relationships warmed up.

It may be easier to avoid unpleasant truths in the short run, but in the long run, better communication invites growth and change. Psychologists Gay and Kathleen Hendricks, authors of many books on relationships, teach the merits of telling the "no-blame truth." Rather than letting little annoyances gather steam, the idea is to mention them before walls build up, as they had between Jack and me.

The art of the no-blame truth, or NBT, as my husband calls it, is kindness. Most of us already know that it's better to comment on a person's behavior and how it makes *you* feel, rather than to attack *their* character. Jack did a good job of telling me how he felt when I ignored him, rather than making me out to be an insensitive snob. A comment such as, "Hey, what am I, a potted plant?" while humorous, would have communicated blame and criticism. The result might have been distance and animosity instead of peace and cooperation. By appealing to my best self, Jack created an opportunity for awareness that I was grateful to have.

Telling the NBT may seem simple, but when you're busy and irritable, your own best self may be temporarily out to lunch. If you let sarcasm, hurt, or anger infiltrate your communications, you risk bringing other people down to the same level. Then everyone suffers and the result that you long for—cooperation, consideration, and peace—becomes less and less probable. This week, pay close attention to the art of truth-in-communication. If your teenager throws clothes all over the house, use the NBT rather than implying that he's a hopeless case who's ruining your life. If your boss is discounting you, make a simple statement about how that makes you feel, without blame or resentment. Clear communication is a cornerstone of intimacy and inner peace.

47. Watch Those Assumptions

When you're in a hurry, it can be easier to make assumptions than it is to communicate. With time, you may come to believe that you're a mind reader who barely has to ask anything at all. And while intuition can be powerful, many assumptions are not examples of it. The only mind that you're reading in many cases may be your own.

My husband, Kurt, and I stumbled over our assumptions out on the golf course one day. He's a great player, while I'm still a rank beginner. I took up the sport so that we could share a relaxing activity. Judging by the number of four-letter words that this simple game elicits from otherwise civilized folk, I have redefined the idea of golf as relaxation. It's a challenging game, but at least it's an absorbing one that affords respite from the usual frustrations of life by providing frustrations all its own. I will never be Tiger Woods, but blasting out of a sand trap can still provide very immediate gratification.

We had just played out a hole. Both balls were nestled happily in the cup, and I was rejoicing in my honest score of seven on a 425-yard par four. Kurt bent down to get our balls and to replace the flag, while I trotted off victorious to the cart. "Hey," he called me back, brandishing my Golden Girls ball. "Don't you want this?"

"Oh," I replied, "I just assumed that you would bring it back to the cart."

He shook his head. "Any *guy* would know that I was waiting to hand him his ball."

We burst out laughing. Both of us had made an assumption: he, that I would know what the customary behavior ought to be; and I, that he would bring the ball back to the cart. This led to a discussion of one his pet names for me: the Queen of Assumptions. He sometimes fits the description of the King of Assumptions. There are no feast days for these familiar saints, but they inhabit the lives of many busy people who worship unknowingly at their shrines.

The busier we get, the more likely it is that we will live in our heads and start to make erroneous assumptions about what other people should know. We know the plan. After all, we thought it all through. Unfortunately, it may not have completed the journey from our brain out our mouth. Our loved ones can find themselves unpleasantly surprised when we announce that we expect them to go to town and do the errands. It makes sense to *us*. We have a report to write this weekend and they're free. They should have known that. Any reasonably conscious person would have figured it out. Even if we didn't mention it explicitly, wouldn't they?

The King and Queen of Assumptions are close relatives of Morris and Mary the Mind Readers. This couple believes that other people are so sensitive and tuned in to them that virtually no communication is necessary. They sometimes preface a complaint with a zinger such as: "If you really cared, you would know that . . ." You can probably fill in the blanks from incidents in your own life such as: "My car was dirty and it would have been nice for you to wash it. . . . I was feeling down and flowers would have made my day. . . . Jennifer needed to be picked up from daycare, and I also had to do the shopping. . . ."

The result of being the King or Queen of Assumptions, and thinking that other people can or should read your mind, is misery. Peace of mind flies out the window when aggravation comes to visit. Expecting someone to read your mind is a form of blaming. Why can't they be more considerate? It's also a symptom of self-absorption. No healthy, balanced person is the sun around which another adult's life revolves. Even in the most loving relationships, partners have their own concerns and constellations of dreams and needs. Love is a partnership involving give-and-take, not a monarchy.

The antidote to mind reading is simple. If you want flowers, learn to ask for them. If it's too hard to both do the shopping and pick up your child from daycare, ask your spouse to choose one of the errands. Clear communication and straightforward requests help keep the peace, and afford other people the respect they deserve.

This week, notice whether you're losing your peace of mind to assumptions. Resolve to communicate clearly, and realize that the busier people are, the more careful you have to be to get their attention before you talk to them. If they're absorbed in something and all you're getting as an answer to your communication is an "Uh-huh," try asking nicely for their complete attention. While this may seem simple and obvious, it's often a stumbling block to communication. Both parties have to be in the here-and-now before minds and hearts can open to make a reasonable and co-creative plan.

48. Spread Civility

❧ ❧

Kindness grows out of a mindful approach to life, when you naturally notice the needs of those around you and give them the respect they deserve. But in our busy lives, rush and worry often narrow the focus of attention. Awareness suffers, and even for those who are naturally kind, compassion sometimes takes a back seat to expediency. When that happens, some of the sweetness leaves life. It's worth making civility a priority so that the kindness that's your own true nature has a chance to blossom and cast its seeds of peace into the world.

Incivility is on the rise, and worse, we've come to expect it. I was dropping off one of my stepsons in Boulder, where he could take a shuttle van to the Denver airport. Since it was cold outside, we waited in the lobby of the hotel that was the pick-up stop. One more passenger waited with us, a high-tech kind of guy who told us that he was on a four-city tour interviewing for a new job. Both of his hands were full of luggage. He had two black wheelies, one of which was topped with a bulky computer case. When the van pulled up, we all headed toward the door.

My stepson Christian and I went to the right, and the "techie" moved left. I held the door for Christian, and as I let it go, it hit the poor man in the face. He had apparently changed directions in mid-course and followed us out. I was mortified and couldn't apologize enough. Even if you think that the coast is clear, it's a good idea to take one last look before letting a killer door have its way.

The man was philosophical. "Think nothing of it. I'm still alive. This sort of thing happens all the time." That's the problem—he's right.

I was at a conference on healing several years ago when a woman rushed up to the podium to make an impassioned announcement before the next speaker began: "We are here at a conference to learn about healing, and healing requires kindness and attention. Two of you just walked through a door without looking to see who was behind you. It hit an elderly woman and knocked her down. If we're too busy to care for one another, we have no business being here."

The busier we are, the less attention we tend to pay to others, and the more irritable and unthinking we can be. This applies not only to strangers, but also to our own family and to the people we work with. Some corporations are so concerned about rude, disrespectful behavior that they're employing a diagnostic tool called the "Organizational Civility Index" to catalog the incidence and type of poor behavior that pollutes the corporate climate and robs employees of peace of mind.

The December 2000 issue of "The National Report on Work & Family" reported on a five-year study conducted at the University of North Carolina (UNC). A whopping 100 percent of the 800 people surveyed reported incivility on the job. Eight-nine percent rated the problem as serious, and more than three-quarters thought that it had increased over the past ten years. The UNC study also looked at the results of rude behavior. More than 50 percent of those surveyed lost work time worrying about an incident that had already happened, or that might happen in the future. Fifty percent considered quitting to avoid a disrespectful co-worker. The offensive behaviors included belittlement, harassment, condescension, insubordination, emotional tirades, discounting of input, damaging rumors, interrupting, and not listening.

Boorish, ill-mannered behavior is getting to be the norm. It's a rare trip to the supermarket when someone hasn't left their cart in the middle of the aisle and blocked traffic, or you aren't sideswiped by a swooping shopper. Most people seem to think nothing of it. When apologies are forthcoming, it's a pleasant surprise indeed. While most of us do our best, almost everyone is occasionally rude. Have you ever failed to listen to a loved one, discounted their opinion, acted condescendingly, or lost it emotionally and started to yell?

This week, monitor your actions for civility and kindness. Be a good listener, and if you ask for someone's input, either use it or tell them why you aren't going to. People need to know that they're respected members of the home or work team. If you're tempted to raise your voice to make a point, take a few deep breaths and count to ten. And when someone slams the door in your face, consider your reply. A curt thank you is condescending and sarcastic, although a distinct temptation.

But when you meet rudeness with more of the same, the problem only escalates. If you have any civil ideas about how to respond to a side-swiping shopper or a hit-and-run door artist, please let me know!

49. Put Love into Action

ॐ ☙

Everyone longs for the same thing: to be loved and to love. The deep sense of connection, worth, and belonging that love provides is as close to heaven as we mortals experience on Earth.

The way that we're parented is the major influence on our capacity for love. Feeling respected and worthwhile as a child provides the foundation for growing in compassion and kindness as an adult. The majority of us get what psychologists think of as "good enough" parenting. Maybe our folks weren't perfect, but at least we grew up with a conscience and the capacity to understand that other people are as important as we are. By the time you're in your 30s, the childhood wounds that block love become obvious. Perhaps you're cynical or afraid of commitment. Maybe you have an uncanny radar that perpetually zeroes in on the wrong kind of friends or lovers. Perhaps you take poor care of yourself or lack the ability to set reasonable boundaries. Maybe you've even lost hope.

If you want peace, eventually you have to commit to a healing process that mends self-concept, teaches emotional intelligence, and helps you to forgive. But not all people have the inner or outer resources to get the emotional healing they need. And some are more seriously wounded. Helping those folks through programs directed toward children, such as Big Brother and Big Sister organizations, homeless shelters, battered women's shelters, and other volunteer agencies is a twofold strategy for peace. You help heal yourself while you offer love and healing to others.

Years ago, Ram Dass wrote a lovely book called *How Can I Help?* He recommended that if you want more inner peace, offering your time and talent for volunteer work will help you get it. As an added bonus, volunteering also improves health and longevity. Many corporations have programs that give workers time off for community service. Giving employees the chance to volunteer on company time turns out to be good business. Workers report feeling more loyalty and job satisfaction because volunteering brings more meaning into their lives. It gives them a chance to put love into action.

My role model for love in action is Robin Casarjian. She is the director of the Lionheart Foundation, which teaches emotional literacy to prisoners. I met her when we were both teaching stress-management programs in Boston. After her book *Forgiveness* was published, Robin got a request to give a lecture on the topic at a local prison. At 9 A.M., 120 out of the 700-member prison population turned out to hear her talk about forgiveness. In her own words, she was "blown away." Some prisoners wanted to do more than just hear about the topic. They wanted to learn how to *do* it. Soon Robin was offering weekly programs in self-healing, forgiveness, and emotional literacy at several prisons.

Rather than addressing the emotional wounds of inmates, prisons are graduate schools in violence. Approximately 1,600 more people are added to the overcrowded prison system every week. You may be surprised that the corrections industry is the fastest-growing sector of the economy. And if we continue at the present rate, over half the population of the United States will be incarcerated by the middle of the century. The way to reverse this trend, of course, lies in helping the children. Unfortunately, our government thinks that we can do it by threatening harsher punishment for adults who are already desperately wounded people. Violence is a self-perpetuating cycle. Abused children turn into adult abusers.

Like all human beings, prisoners yearn to make sense of their lives and to create a future different from their past. But without love and self-respect, change is impossible. Using stress-management skills, cognitive reframing, meditation, role-playing, and self-reflection, Robin teaches prisoners how to understand their feelings and express them in a mature, con-structive way. The core of her program is forgiveness, which is also the cornerstone of taking responsibility for their actions.

In order to reach more prisoners, Robin put her program into book form. *Houses of Healing* has been distributed free to all federal and state prisons in the United States. The title reflects Robin's dream that prisons will be transformed from schools of violence into houses of healing. Workbooks and videos for people who want to teach the program are available (for information, go to **www.Lionheart.org**), and the pro-gram is offered in many correctional institutions across the country. In a short yet moving video about men and women in Houses of Healing programs, there's a shot of sweet-faced children playing. Robin's narrative asks the poignant question: "How did they come into the world as beautiful, divine chil-dren; and how is it that they ended up in prison?" There, but for the power of love, could go any one of us.

This week, think about how you can put love into action. The problems in our society may seem overwhelming, but if each one of us helps, we can make a difference. Mother Teresa was once asked how she managed to pick up more than 40,000 dying people from the streets of Calcutta. She replied that if she thought about them all, she would have been over-whelmed. But it happened gradually. She picked them up one at a time. She called this the law of "one-by-one." This is the way that love heals, and it's a strategy that anyone can adopt.

PART VI

Strategies for Creating Wisdom and Purpose in Your Life

50. Find Meaning in Your Life

The human longing to make sense of the past and to build a better future is a force of nature every bit as powerful as wind and fire. People seek meaning for their lives everywhere—from fortune cookies to psychic hotlines. But a peaceful person's desire for a happy future runs deeper than a superficial craving for wealth or fame. We want to know that there's a worthwhile purpose to our brief existence that serves life. A sense of meaning makes our time precious and helps us weather life's storms, growing from adversity rather than feeling powerless or victimized.

The critical difference between those who grow from difficult circumstances and those who don't is the ability of the former to find some positive meaning in their misfortune. During the years I practiced medical psychology, I had the privilege of observing how that transformational process could change the course of people's lives. The passion to help my patients in their search for meaning was an outgrowth of a personal tragedy and the powerful need to make sense of it.

My father had died during the years when I was a cancer cell biologist, working in the laboratory. One of the drugs that kept his leukemia in check had a terrible side effect. It made him manic to the point of insanity. Under its destructive influence, he was totally unlike his former kind and patient self. It was as if an aggressive stranger had moved into his broken body. My family tried to talk to the doctor about it, but all that we got was a canned lecture about the need to continue the treatment because it was lifesaving. The quality of life didn't seem to matter.

After a year of treatment, my father was taken off the drug in preparation for surgery. For a few sweet weeks, he was himself again. It was like discovering that your dearest love, lost during a storm at sea, had floated safely into port. The time we had with him during that brief respite was poignant because we knew that the very drug that killed his soul gave life to his ailing body. To live, he would have to take it once again.

The drug was the devil's own bargain. It is a true shame, and I believe, a violation of the Hippocratic Oath, when a physician fails to help a family cope with such a horrible circumstance. My father's doctor, a noted expert in leukemia, seemed blind to everything about his patient except blood counts. He offered neither emotional nor spiritual help. So, back in his right mind, my father made what must have been an excruciating choice. In the wee hours of a hot September morning, he jumped out of the window of the high-rise apartment in Florida where he and my mother had retired. He chose to take his own life rather than going back on the drug.

My mother was inconsolable. Over and over again she wondered why she hadn't seen the suicide coming. I think that she would willingly have laid down her own life for the man that she had loved those many years. As a result of her soul-wrenching guilt, she became a hermit and cut off contact with her friends. Unable to find a higher meaning in the tragedy, my mother lived in a self-imposed exile for 13 years until her own death.

At the time of my father's suicide, I was a medical scientist trying to find a cure for cancer. I knew volumes about the biology of tumor cells, but almost nothing about the human response to the illness. The choice between quality of life and quantity of life had been just one more academic issue. Then it hit home with the destructive force of a heat-seeking missile.

Like my mother, I suffered from crippling guilt. As a medical researcher, I felt that it should have been possible to give my dad safe passage through the medical maze. Instead, he died on my watch. It seemed a particularly dark irony. But with time, I began to look for a higher meaning in the tragedy. His death was part of a chain of events that culminated in my leaving the laboratory and living my passion. I had always wanted to study the connection between mind and body. And now I longed to bring the soul back into medicine.

As a result of our family's tragedy, my first project in the field of behavioral medicine was to set up mind/body groups for people with cancer. If just one family had an outcome better than ours, I believed that it would give meaning to my father's death. The work was a kind of redemption. I saw his face in everyone that I cared for. I saw my mother's face in that of each suffering spouse. Rather than considering his death a failure, or a meaningless heartbreak, I began to think of it as a calling. Families coping with cancer were my main vocation for many years.

It's a strange and wonderful thing, this being human. It's often during the hardest times, rather than the most peaceful ones, that you find a purpose that gives meaning to your days so that your life becomes a blessing. The passion born of meaning is more than a psychological breakthrough or an emotional coping strategy. It's a glimpse into the soul that elevates life's predictable hardships into sacred quests. Every action born of higher meaning becomes like a prayer, and obstacles to living your purpose part like the Red Sea before a Higher Power.

This week, find two or three hours when you can count on being alone. Write down the story of your life as if it were a novel. Remember that the story is not so much in the events that happened, as it is in the meaning you give them. While the past is over, remember that your story is always open to revision. To *revise* literally means to "see again." Seeing your story from the vantage point of the soul can change your future for the better, no matter what the past may have been.

51. Get Your Priorities in Order

❦❦

Even when life is blessed with meaning and purpose, it can still be tough to keep your priorities straight. Loving what you do can lead to doing it with so much gusto that life gets busier than ever. But if you let your work come before family, friends, and self-care, inner peace can evaporate quickly.

People who participate in 12-step recovery programs have a pithy slogan: "First Things First." Following that plan keeps life's important priorities from being buried in the sand by the incoming tide of daily responsibilities.

I once heard an inspiring story about keeping your priorities straight. Unfortunately, I don't know the source, but I appreciate the wisdom of the person who told it. It concerned a 75-year-old man who was giving advice to a young father so busy that he had missed his daughter's dance recital. Those moments are precious, and as you look back on your life, they are the things that shine. Children grow up in the blink of an eye, and the season for dance recitals and soccer games soon passes. Perhaps you meant to go, but there never seemed to be enough time.

The older man talked about a discovery he had made in his 55th year. He realized that if he lived an average life span of 75 years, he had only 1,000 Saturdays left. The story caught my interest, since I'm also 55. Sure enough, if I live another 19 or 20 years, that makes just about 1,000 Saturdays.

Anyway, the man bought 1,000 marbles, which he put in a clear plastic jar. Every Saturday he took one out and threw it away. As he watched the number dwindle, life seemed more precious, and his priorities became more clear. As a result, he spent more time with his loved ones.

It turned out that the very morning that he had shared this story with the busy young father, he had taken the last marble out of the jar. We are all losing our marbles, he concluded philosophically, but when you see them disappearing, you understand that life is finite. Each day is a gift and can't be taken for granted. But most of us do just that.

In the great Hindu classic, the Bhagavad Gita, the god Krishna, who is disguised as a charioteer, asks a question of Arjuna, the young warrior whom he's helping. Krishna asks, "What is the greatest wonder on the earth?" The answer is our denial of death. Even though we see friends, family, famous people, and strangers dying all the time, we don't seem to realize that death will come for us as well.

I've decided to buy some marbles of my own to help me remember. I'm going to buy pretty ones, the cat's-eye variety that we played with as kids. And I'm going to put them in a graceful glass vase on the dining room table. That way I'll see them often and remember that every day is a gift. But I'll keep each Saturday's discard for fun, rather than tossing it out. It's never too early to have a second childhood.

This week, think about your top three daily priorities. Maybe family time, visiting with friends, prayer, eating your six servings of fruits and vegetables, exercise, or study are on your list. Get a glass jar and some marbles. Don't worry, you won't need 1,000; just 21 will do the trick. Every time you carry through with one of your priorities, put a marble in the jar. At the end of a week, if all 21 are in there, you'll know that you succeeded in honoring your three most important priorities every day. If there are fewer than 21 and you need more inspiration to keep first things first, you might want to buy 1,000 more marbles and start the Saturday countdown.

52. Keep the Faith

🐦🐦

Scholars and theologians spin endless theories about where we came from, why we're here, where we're going, and what's going to happen to us when we get there. But in the end, the meaning of life is a matter of faith. And faith can be a fragile bird whose wings are easily torn, or a mighty eagle that soars above you. It can guide you on your journey and bring you peace even when the path before you is obscure or strewn with obstacles. In the end, faith is less a set of beliefs than your willingness to surrender to a mysterious force of love and guidance that helps you find your way.

During the years when I was a medical psychologist, I had the opportunity to hear a lot about faith, since being ill or facing death tends to bring existential questions to the fore. Faith turned out to be a very personal thing for most people, far richer than an unquestioned internalization of religious dogma. Talking to a young mother in her 30s with two small children and advanced Hodgkins disease taught me a lot about faith. "Susan" wanted desperately to live and watch her children grow up. She did everything she could to ensure her recovery. Not only was she cared for by excellent physicians, but she also took responsibility for eating well, attending our mind/body clinic, and consulting a Chinese physician for acupuncture and treatment with herbs.

"I'm doing all I can to fight for my life and my children," she told me, "but the outcome is up to God. Like most people who are sick, I pray to be healed. But I know that's not always part of the bigger picture. I'm not narcissistic enough to believe that God runs the universe based on my suggestions. So I also pray for the strength and courage to follow God's plan with a peaceful heart, whether it means life or death. The universe is so much larger, grander, and more loving than anything we could imagine. Everything unfolds with such elegance, in its own time. That's what I have faith in. That's what comforts me when I wake up sick and scared."

Susan loved a story about faith that the assistant director of our program, Steve Maurer, told her group. It was a close reflection of her philosophy. The story concerns a humble advisor to a powerful king. The advisor was a learned man who had studied philosophy in the great cities of the East, yet he led his life according to a simple rule of faith: "Don't worry. Everything happens for the best."

One day the king was out hunting, and the regal stag he had been tracking for several seasons got away again. He was so frustrated that he broke his great bow in two against a rock. His advisor, ever philosophical, reassured him that everything happens for the best. Sick of hearing what he thought was an inane platitude from a stupid philosopher, the king had the advisor locked up in the dungeon. "*Now* tell me that everything happens for the best," he challenged.

But the advisor only shook his head and smiled. "We'll see," he said, as he settled down on the stone floor of his cell, pulling his cloak up against him to ward off the cold.

The following day, the king went hunting again, alone this time since his advisor was in the dungeon. While jumping over a pile of brush, he was thrown from his stallion and broke his leg. A band of hostile men rode up shortly, and the helpless king cringed in terror as they set upon him. He was sure that he would be robbed and killed, or kidnaped and held for ransom. But oddly, gesticulating excitedly at his broken leg, the men got on their horses and rode away.

The king managed to mount his steed and return to the castle, although he was in great pain. As soon as the court physician had set his leg, the angry king called for his advisor be brought from the dungeon. "Tell me now," he growled menacingly at the man, "how breaking my leg was all for the best." Crossing his massive arms over his crimson robes, the king reclined with a sour smirk on his pained face.

"By your leave, Your Majesty, I will explain exactly why everything happened for the best. Those were not bandits who set upon you, but worshipers of the nature gods. It is spring, their time of sacrifice. They were hoping to capture you as an offering to their deities so that the crops would grow well this year, and their flocks would multiply. But since your leg was broken, you were useless to them. Sacrifices must be perfect specimens."

The king considered this answer, remembering the way that the men had pointed at his leg with such excitement. "That may be true enough," he said to the advisor, "but how can it be all for the best that you were thrown in the dungeon?"

"Think about it," suggested the advisor. "I always go hunting with you. When the barbarians left you because your leg was broken, they would have taken me instead. Even as we speak, I would have been sacrificed to their gods. So being locked up in the dungeon saved my life."

❧☙

Whether or not you're religious, faith is a major component of inner peace. Dr. James Fowler, of the Harvard Divinity School, wrote a wonderful book called *Stages of Faith*. He traces six stages through which faith matures, as we grow psychologically throughout the life span. Faith passes through the black-and-white, heaven-and-hell stage typical of early childhood, beyond the shared religious convictions of family and peers, to an independent consideration of our place in the universe. The final stage, which Fowler calls Universalizing Faith, is based on compassionate respect for all people and the determination to make the world a better place. People such as Mohandas Gandhi, Martin Luther King, Jr., the Dalai Lama,

Rabbi Abraham Heschel, and Mother Teresa have entirely different religious convictions, but they're alike in modeling the highest stage of faith, which finds its expression through enlightened social action.

This week, take an hour or two and write a spiritual autobiography. What are the stages that your own faith has progressed through? When you're busy and hassled or are experiencing serious problems, does your faith support you? Does it comfort you, and what are the sources of the peace it brings? Alternatively, you may discover that some of your religious beliefs frighten you or seem nonsensical, and that it's time to reconsider them. Or perhaps faith is an elusive thing, in which case it's well worth pursuing.

If you gather a small group of family and friends together to do this exercise and then compare your reflections, you'll be amazed what you can learn from one another. At one seminar I facilitated, a mother and daughter who were both Catholic attended together. During a small group discussion, they were astonished to find that they had completely different experiences of their religion, and that their faith stemmed from separate roots. In comparing their journeys, both were enriched, while developing an even deeper respect for one another and their religion.

ல ல ல

Closing Thoughts:
A Vision for the Future

Y ou picked up this book because of your hope that you could find inner peace in a world gone mad with busyness. It is my hope, as well. If you long to create a future different from your past, then you're a member of a growing group of people who hold a collective vision for peace that can change society and make the world a better place for everyone.

If any of the 52 lessons in this book were a source of inspiration and reflection for you, I hope that you're putting them into action. I've been in the field of personal growth for more than 20 years, and am well aware of the tendency to learn something, think of it as valuable, and then promptly forget all about it. I kept the essays purposely short so that you can reread them often and put their message to work in your life. You might want to check back through the table of contents and choose the five entries that made the greatest impression on you. These make a good starting point for creating a new future.

Remember that change doesn't happen all at once (unless you're in the Witness Protection Program). Small steps will get you where you're going. And if you take honest steps toward peace, I can almost guarantee that you'll go to places more extraordinary than you could have ever imagined. There's a divine hand that works unseen. If you take a single step toward positive change, that divine energy will take a hundred steps toward *you*. New worlds and unbelievable possibilities will open up for you. The synchronicities that will begin appearing in your life will become a source of delight and amazement.

One strong suggestion I have for working with this book is to buy a few copies for friends and family and start an Inner Peace Group. You can discuss a new essay each week, and compare notes on how you're putting the previous week's material into action. Margaret Meade believed that cultural change would come less from legislation and big social programs than it would from small groups of committed people meeting in living rooms. I agree. If we are to create a new future, the power to do so is magnified exponentially wherever two or more of us gather for a good purpose.

Remember the basics: breathe, take time for a walk, take care of yourself, be a good listener, practice gratitude, forgive, search for meaning, learn to manage your mind, keep things simple, and practice a few random acts of kindness.

Together, we can change the world.

∽ ∽ ∽

Resources

Your Inner Peace Kit

This book is one of four parts to an Inner Peace Kit, which I designed to appeal to all your sensory modes of learning for the most complete support of peace, relaxation, creativity, and healing. The other three components are a home video of the Public Television program based on the book, an abridged version the book (read by me) on tape, and a CD of classical music compiled in partnership with international music and healing expert Don Campbell, whose work you read about in essay #14.

1. **Book:** *Inner Peace for Busy People: 52 Simple Strategies for Transforming Your Life*

2. **Home Video:** *Inner Peace for Busy People: Simple Strategies for Transforming Your Life.* The video features my Public Television pledge special, along with special bonus material covering additional topics.

3. **Audio Program:** *Inner Peace for Busy People: Simple Strategies for Transforming Your Life.* This is an audio program in which I read selected entries from the book. It can transform driving time, or any time, into an opportunity for learning, peace, and inspiration. The audio program makes the lessons personal, as if I'm speaking just to you.

4. **Music:** *Inner Peace for Busy People: Music to Relax and Renew.* This is a very special selection of nine carefully chosen pieces of classical music on a CD compiled by Don Campbell and me. It was produced especially to reduce stress and allow the inner peace of your own authentic self to emerge. The CD promotes a feeling of spaciousness, awareness, and inspiration that can make every day more peaceful and creative. The CD was produced by Spring Hill Media, which also carries a fine line of other inspiring, healing music that is one of the best selections available anywhere—go to **www.springhillmedia.com**; write Spring Hill Media, P.O. Box 800, Boulder, CO 80306 for a catalog; or phone (303) 938-1188.

You can purchase all of the components of the Inner Peace Kit directly through Hay House at **www.hayhouse.com**, or by calling (800) 654-5126. Hay House maintains a complete inventory of my other books and audio programs as well.

A Musical Journey for Busy People

You can get more information about the power of music to aid learning, creativity, healing, and relaxation through Don Campbell's organization, the Mozart Effect Resource Center. You can write care of: The Mozart Effect, P.O. Box 4179, Boulder, CO, 80306; go on-line at **www.MozartEffect.com**, or phone (303) 440-8046. Don's CDs, books, and other important information is also available through the Center.

The following musical journey is designed to guide you in listening to our *Inner Peace for Busy People* CD. Even without the music, the affirmations for each track are a reminder of what you've learned in this book. Since music activates the limbic system of the brain and accesses emotions, reading the suggested affirmations slowly, while feeling their spirit in the music, will help anchor peace, awareness, and creativity more firmly in your life.

Whenever you need to relax and restore yourself, to find inspiration or lift your spirits, the music will be there for you—internally as well as externally. Music—perhaps more than any other external experience—has the power to bring you home to yourself.

The *Inner Peace* music CD consists of the nine selections outlined below. The affirmations for the musical journey are meant to accompany each piece. Really take some time to experience what's written so that you can feel it deeply in your body and emotions.

Music reveals itself to you more deeply with repeated listening. So, the first few times you relax with the CD, simply listen to familiarize yourself with the music and let it become a part of you. As Don Campbell says, "Realize that you are on a ship of sound that is passing by different landscapes."

You might wish to center yourself in your breathing as you begin to listen. Pay close attention to each in-breath and out-breath, as if you were riding the tides. Give yourself to the flow of breath, and let it carry you effortlessly toward your center. Notice that after you've exhaled, there is a tiny moment in time before the next breath flows in. That little space between the breaths is perfectly quiet and calm. One moment has passed away, and the next has yet to begin. As you pay attention to this place of infinite possibility, it will expand, drawing you deeper and deeper into your center.

As you listen, stay in that peaceful center, and let the music carry you home to your soul as you consider the seed thought, or affirmation, that accompanies each piece.

Track 1: *The Lark Ascending,*
by Ralph Vaughan Williams (15:08 minutes)
My mind is as spacious as the clear blue sky. Thoughts pass by like clouds, drifting through the sky of pure mind. I can identify with the vastness of the sky, rather than the clouds. While the clouds are ever-changing, the sky of pure mind is eternal, creative, wise, peaceful, and connected to all that is. I am rising on the wings of the soul, like a lark ascending.

Track 2: *Berceuse, Opus 116,* by Gabriel Fauré
(3:33 minutes)
My body, mind, and spirit are forms of divine energy. As I let go and relax, my energy comes into harmony with a greater flow. I can float on the sea of sound, cradled in a warm cocoon, letting melody restore the rhythm of my body, heal me, and return me to peace.

Track 3: *Lute Concerto in D Major—Largo,*
by Antonio Vivaldi (5:48 minutes)
I am dancing through space. Everything is in me, and I am in everything. The breath is my center, my anchor, as I experience the song of the spheres from the safety of my true self.

Track 4: *Symphony No. 35 in C Major—Andante,*
by Wolfgang Amadeus Mozart (4:26 minutes)
I am infused with divine energy, strong, peaceful, coherent as a laser, and completely aware. I am clear, compassionate, and ready to act. All the help I need is coming to me, inspiring and supporting the most creative use of my gifts and talents.

Track 5: *Concerto Opus 9, No. 6 in G Major for Two Oboes—Allegro,* **by Tomaso Giovanni Albinoni** (3:17 minutes)
I am inspired and energized, filled with gratitude for the many opportunities to love, live, and create. I can accomplish anything when I am in this space of infinite awareness and unlimited possibility.

Track 6: *Concerto Opus 7, No. 9 in F Major for Oboe— Allegro,* **by Tomaso Giovanni Albinoni** (2:36 minutes)
I am fully alive and aware. I am awake to the creative impulses that are even now unfolding within me and all around me.

Track 7: *Concerto Opus 7, No. 1 in D Major for Oboe— Allegro Assai,* **by Tomas Giovanni Albinoni** (2:03 minutes)
Inspired and grateful, I am filled with passion and purpose. My life has meaning. Strong and resilient, everything I need for success is already within me.

Track 8: *Piano Concerto No. 1—Romance/Larghetto,* **by Frédéric Chopin** (9:18 minutes)
I am a child of the universe, filled with wonder and possibility, compassion and lovingkindness. Part of the song of life, I am unique and beautiful. My life is an offering, a gift, in tune with all other lives. We are all relations, each the lover and the beloved.

Track 9: *Piano Concerto No. 3 in C Minor—Largo,* **by Ludwig van Beethoven** (9:51 minutes)
I see the spirit in all things—from the tiniest atom to the majesty of the star-kissed universe. The same spirit that keeps the planets in their orbit, and the sun on its course, is present in me.

Other Books and Audiocassettes by Joan Borysenko

Books:

I have written ten books in the fields of psychology, mind/body medicine, women's health, and spirituality. People at seminars often ask me to explain a little bit about each one, including the order in which they were written. They are listed in chronological order below, with a brief description:

Minding the Body, Mending the Mind, Addison Wesley, 1987 (hardcover); Bantam, 1988 (tradepaper). This *New York Times* bestseller is a classic in mind/body medicine, as useful today as it was when it was first published. You can read more about learning to manage your mind, meditation, breathing, reframing, optimism and pessimism, and using mental imagery. Simple and accessible, it includes a self-assessment of your stress levels and physical symptoms so that you can keep track of your improvement.

Guilt is the Teacher, Love is the Lesson, Warner Books, 1990. This is a book about healing childhood wounds and finding spiritual meaning in your life. If you feel guilty, are afraid of anger, are a perfectionist, or have an excessive need to please people, this book will help you heal, and move into your authentic self. It is also excellent for those people who have been wounded by religious fear and guilt.

On Wings of Light: Meditations for Awakening to the Source (with artist Joan Drescher), Warner Books,1992. This is a beautiful, large-format book of meditations and affirmations that can inspire both adults and children.

Fire in the Soul: A New Psychology of Spiritual Optimism,
Warner Books,1993. This is my favorite of the books I've
written, because of the many thank-you letters I've received
over the years. If you're wrestling with questions of faith,
seeking spiritual guidance, or coping with a difficult life situation, this book can bring tremendous insight and comfort. I think of it as a lifeline in troubling times and a book
about faith for all times. I have been told often that it can
save your life.

The Power of the Mind to Heal (with Myron Borysenko), Hay
House, 1994. I wrote this book to capture the workshop
information and practical exercises that my former husband and I developed together. It's also available as a best-
selling audiocassette program from Nightingale-Conant
(see page 169).

Pocketful of Miracles, Warner Books, 1995. This book is a spiritual companion and guide based on the wisdom of many
different cultures and religious traditions. It has an entry
for each day of the year, keyed to the natural world, cycles,
seasons, and holy days. Each daily entry consists of a seed
thought for contemplation; and a prayer, practice, or meditation for the day.

*A Woman's Book of Life: The Biology, Psychology and Spiritual-
ity of the Feminine Lifecycle,* Riverhead Press, 1997. This is a
book for every woman, tracing the fullness of our development through the life span. Written when I was 49 years old
and coming into the wisdom years, this book provides a
fresh slant on menopause, aging, intuition, and the way
that we continue to grow through every cycle of our lives.

7 Paths to God, Hay House, 1997. (This book was first published in a hardcover edition as *The Ways of the Mystic;* we changed the title of the paperback to *7 Paths to God*.) Every person is different biologically, hardwired for the journey to God in a unique way. The major spiritual paths—from creativity and nature to meditation and ethics—are covered, with practical suggestions for walking your path.

A Woman's Journey to God: Finding the Feminine Path, Riverhead Books, 2000. All major religions were founded for men, geared to their unique biology and way of understanding the world. In this breakthrough book, I show how women can develop a spiritual path of our own. When male and female ways are both honored, we will have a true, living spirituality and a more peaceful world.

Audio Programs:

Three types of audio programs are available: lecture programs, audio books, and guided meditations:

Lectures

- *How to Overcome Life's Problems* (two-tape set), Hay House

- *Healing and Spirituality: The Sacred Quest for Transformation of Body and Soul* (two-tape set), Hay House

- *Pathways to God: A Dialogue Between Joan Borysenko, Ph.D., and Deepak Chopra, M.D.* (two-tape set), Hay House

- *Reflections on A Woman's Book of Life* (one tape), Hay House

- *The Beginner's Guide to Meditation* (two-tape set), Hay House

- *Seventy Times Seven: On the Spiritual Art of Forgiveness* (two-tape set), Sounds True

- *The Power of the Mind to Heal* (six-tape set), Nightingale-Conant

- *Your Spiritual Quest* (six-tape set), Nightingale-Conant

Audio Books

The following books are read by me, and are unabridged:

- *Minding the Body, Mending the Mind* (Hay House)
- *7 Paths to God* (Hay House)

Meditation Series

- *Meditations for Relaxation and Stress Reduction*
- *Meditations for Self-Healing and Inner Power*
- *Meditations for Forgiveness*
- *Meditations for Overcoming Depression*
- *Meditations for Healing the Inner Child and Lovingkindness*
- *Invocation of the Angels*
- *Morning and Evening Meditations and Prayers*

Website Info

Please check my Website at: **www.joanborysenko.com** for information on Inner Peace Groups; the itinerary for my seminars and lectures; articles; and news on mind/body medicine, psychology, and spirituality. You can also sign up for my free e-mail newsletter and find links to many worthwhile organizations.

ℒ ℒ ℒ

ᴄᴀ ᴀ ᴄᴀ

About the Author

Joan Borysenko, Ph.D., is one of the leading experts on
stress, spirituality, and the mind/body connection. She has a
doctorate in medical sciences from Harvard Medical School, is
a licensed clinical psychologist, and is the co-founder and
former director of the Mind/Body Clinical Programs at the Beth
Israel Deaconess Medical Center, Harvard Medical School.
Currently the president of Mind/Body Health Sciences, Inc., she
is an internationally known speaker and consultant in women's
health and spirituality, integrative medicine, and the
mind/body connection. She is the author of ten books, including the *New York Times* bestseller *Minding the Body, Mending the
Mind*. Joan's Website is: **JoanBorysenko.com**.

ᴄᴀ ᴀ ᴄᴀ